THE ART
of
BREAKFAST

Copyright text and photos
©2011 by Dana Moos

ISBN: 978-0-892-72940-1

Library of Congress Cataloging-in-Publication Data

Moos, Dana.
The art of breakfast : how to bring B & B
entertaining home / Dana Moos.
p. cm.
Includes index.
ISBN 978-0-89272-940-1
1. Breakfasts. 2. Entertaining. I. Title.
TX733.M664 2011
642--dc22
2011003098

Design by Miroslaw Jurek
and Jennifer Baum.
Set in Esta.
Printed in China

5 4 3 2 1

Down East
Books • Magazine • Online
www.downeast.com
Distributed to the trade
by National Book Network

CLASSIC POPOVERS,
page 104

the art of breakfast

How to Bring B&B Entertaining Home

DANA MOOS

Down East

OATMEAL CAKE,
page 38

To my husband,
Greg, who believed in me enough to leave the
security of the job he held for more than twenty
years, and head to Maine to buy a bed and breakfast.
Thank you so much for just letting me do my thing!
And for being so patient when it comes to taking
pictures of the food before we eat: "Will we be eating
this while it's hot?" And for always being a step
behind me to do my dishes. But mostly for being
by my side. It's the little things that matter
the most, and I appreciate them all.

To my friends and family who have always been
supportive and encouraging and know I'm happy to
cook for them any time. Thanks to Mom and Dad for
introducing me to fine foods at a young age; I may
not have fully appreciated it then, but I do now!

And many thanks to our former inn guests who
always encouraged me to write a cookbook, who
asked for recipes, and took photos of our breakfasts.
You've been an inspiration over the years.

Thank you all!

With much love, Dana

POACHED EGGS SERVED
IN ROASTED TOMATO,
page 78

CONTENTS

INTRODUCTION

Like many, I find great joy and gratification in cooking and providing for guests. So much so that in 2004 my husband and I moved from Washington, D.C. to Mount Desert Island to buy the Kingsleigh Inn in Southwest Harbor. Once there, helping to enhance my guests' vacations was extremely satisfying. Especially when it came to the food. Because our inn was too small to serve dinner (not to mention too busy without additional hired help), I pushed the envelope when it came to gourmet three-course breakfasts. My feeling was that breakfast could be as special as fine dining in the evening.

Over my five years as innkeeper, I learned techniques to make things simple and easy to prepare in advance. But more importantly I learned how to make breakfast artful. Now when I walk through a food market, the shelves are filled with food to paint my canvas or empty plate. Fresh fruits and vegetables are my preferred medium. Butter, cream, and sugar are a close second. My favorite kitchen tool is a torch (and not a mini-torch, I'm talking a real one used for plumbing jobs).

This book is about transforming sophisticated gourmet into everyday simplicity. It's about creating beautiful art on a plate by combining fresh fruits and vegetables in imaginative, yet simple ways. It's about seeing food in colors, the way we learned from the color chart in elementary school. It's about looking at a plate of food as a composition and balancing colors, textures, and flavors. We don't just eat with our mouths, we eat with our eyes and our nose. When you begin to appreciate food in this manner, you'll be able to grasp the basic principles of the art component of creating a fine dining experience during any meal.

When you create for friends and family, you share a bit of yourself. This is what I learned and most appreciated as an innkeeper; the art of providing and caretaking. Something else I learned as an innkeeper is that you can't please all of the people all of the time. But I sure tried. I catered to vegetarians, low-carb diets, gluten-free diets, egg allergies, lactose intolerance, you name it. I wanted everyone to like everything I made! So when I created my menus, some days might have been heavy on the butter and sugar, but others big on vegetables and low on carbs. Carnivores didn't even realize I rarely served meat because what they were enjoying was so much more creative and fresh. What I ended up with was something that I've been saying for years: everything in moderation. That's exactly what you'll find in this cookbook: equal parts indulgence and moderation, never compromising taste, quality, or creativity.

So dig in. You'll find this book to be part epicurian education, recipe collection, food photography — but most of all, a tool to inspire and spark your own culinary creativity. Hopefully, you, your friends, and your family will enjoy what you'll learn on your journey with *The Art of Breakfast*. Bon appetit!

—*Dana Moos*

CHAPTER 1

Fruit Course

Grapefruit Brûlée *with* Vanilla Bean Crème

This dish was a Condé Nast travel writer favorite. I've enjoyed broiled grapefruit at many bed and breakfasts, but the sugar tends to melt before it broils, not allowing you to achieve a nice thick sugar crust. Using a torch gives you control of the burning. For those on cholesterol medication who can't eat grapefruit, orange slices bruléed with Vanilla Bean Crème *(page 141)* taste just like an orange Creamsicle.

Serves 4

2 ruby red grapefruits
8 tablespoons Vanilla Bean Crème *(page 141)*
8 tablespoons light brown sugar

I. Halve each grapefruit and section with a grapefruit knife or tool. (I have a fabulous two-sided knife with a double blade that cuts along each side of the membrane. The other curved end cuts the fruit from the rind.) Place 2 tablespoons of the Vanilla Bean Crème on top of each grapefruit half.

2. Sprinkle 2 tablespoons sugar over the sauce on each half and torch immediately. Work quickly to avoid the sugar dissolving before being torched. You may need to layer more sugar and torch again in order to get the right burn.

Dana's Tip

Don't do as I do: I learned that my glass dishes were not flameproof on the last morning of our third season at the inn. I had sixteen bowls with grapefruit halves, ready for the torching. I usually topped two at a time with sugar and then torched. I got to the second-to-last dish and as I held the torch, apparently I must have held the flame too close to the glass and it cracked and went all over the kitchen island and shattered glass was tossed around, into the bowls of ready-to-be-served fruit. Needless to say, I didn't serve a fruit course that morning, we went right into the entrée. That next season I bought new flameproof dishes!

Grilled Peaches *with* Raspberry Sorbet

This is my version of Peach Melba—the cool sorbet against the warm grilled peach is delicious! On warm days I served the peaches chilled. I equally enjoy sliced and grilled pineapple, particularly chilled the next day, since there's time for the juice and grilled flavor to meld. Drizzle it over vanilla frozen yogurt and there's another fruit course or light dessert. Add a dollop of Nutella and call it heaven!

Serves 4

4 medium-ripe large peaches

4 tablespoons toasted walnut oil (I love Fiore oils, but you can use any brand)

2 tablespoons granulated sugar

2 teaspoons white peach balsamic vinegar (or use a white balsamic)

Raspberry Coulis (page 137), for garnish

Raspberry Sorbet (page 30)

1. Halve and pit the peaches.

2. Drizzle the oil over the peach halves and dust with the sugar.

3. Grill the peaches over medium heat, flat side down, until you see some grill marks and char, about 10 minutes. Remove from the grill and place in container to rest for a couple of minutes. Evenly drizzle the vinegar while the peaches are still warm.

4. Drizzle the plate with Raspberry Coulis. Serve with a scoop of Raspberry Sorbet.

Watermelon and Kiwi *with* Coconut Lime Crème

This is one of the classic examples of fruits of opposite colors working beautifully together. The inspiration came from the use of lime and coconut in Thai foods. The lime adds such a delightful brightness to the dish and won't curdle the sour cream. I wanted to use a fruit of the opposite color to the watermelon and experimented with kiwi. I just had a feeling it was going to work. The kiwi is very acidic, the watermelon not as much; the sauce marries the two beautifully.

Serves 6

$^1/_2$ of a medium seedless watermelon (or a whole baby seedless melon)

8 kiwi

juice and zest of 1 lime

$^1/_2$ cup Coconut Lime Cream *(page 140)*

1. Cut the rind from the watermelon and kiwis. Cut the watermelon into triangles about $^1/_4$ inch thick and about the size of an oversized tortilla chip. Cut the kiwi into $^1/_4$ inch thick slices. Refrigerate both until well chilled, about 45 minutes.

2. When ready to serve, stack on a dry plate, starting with watermelon, alternating fruits. Squeeze about a teaspoon of lime juice onto each stack of fruit, then spoon a few tablespoons of the Coconut Lime Cream over the top of the stack and onto the plate.

3. Garnish with a sprinkling of lime zest (pass the lime over the zester twice).

Pineapple Banana Cairns
with Cinnamon Crème

I clearly recall the very first dish I created for the inn's menu before we even moved to Maine. I put sliced bananas and pineapple in a flameproof dish, sprinkled cinnamon, topped it with brown sugar, and broiled for a couple minutes. When I realized that I had no control over the browning, my husband pulled out his torch. My pineapple and banana towers were born. But guests Noreen and Michael one morning claimed that they looked like cairns, the directional rock stacks that serve as hiking trail markers in nearby Acadia National Park. From that morning on, we put them on our regular menu and called them Pineapple Banana Cairns.

Serves 4

½ of a pineapple, peeled and cut into vertical quarters

2 ripe bananas

4 tablespoons light brown sugar

4 tablespoons Cinnamon Crème *(page 141)*

I. Cut the core off of each of the four pineapple quarters. Slice two of the pineapple quarters and both bananas into about ten ¼ inch thick slices. Layer, starting with the largest slices of pineapple on the bottom, stacking four pieces of each.

2. Top the tower with a tablespoon of sauce, then a tablespoon of sugar.

3. Carefully torch at a distance that will allow the sugar to burn evenly. This takes about 4 to 5 seconds (depending on the size of your flame) if the flame is about 2 to 3 inches from the sugar. You're looking for the sugar crystals to melt and then lightly burn. If they dissolve into the sauce before you can burn them, just layer another teaspoon of sugar and quickly torch again. You may have to adjust how close you hold the flame to the sugar. Also keep the flame moving all over the sugar to avoid a hot spot. If the sugar starts to smoke, you may have just gone a microsecond too long and will end up with burned sugar. But you can just remove the sugar and start over! Just practice, it will take some getting used to, but it's worth it.

Dana's Tip

You're trying to melt the sugar with the flame before it starts to naturally dissolve in the wet sauce. You also want to ensure all sugar crystals are melted and meld together, which then allows the top surface of the sugar to burn and brown. The sugar crystals when melted and then burnt will essentially become a solid piece of hard candy and not individual crystals. White sugar will not work as the crystals are too small and will immediately dissolve in the sauce before you can even turn the torch on.

Vanilla Bean Panna Cotta *with* Berries

This is a basic recipe that can be flavored a variety of ways. My twist is the addition of cream cheese. I used to serve this vanilla-flavored version with Raspberry Coulis *(page 137)*, fresh raspberries, and blueberries on the Fourth of July at the inn. I used mini bundt tins so that when turned out onto a plate they had a nice decorative look. You could also use individual ramekins.

Serves 8

1 envelope unflavored gelatin

2 tablespoons cold water

1½ cups heavy cream

¾ cup half and half

⅓ cup plus 1 tablespoon granulated sugar

4 ounces cream cheese, room temperature

1 vanilla bean (or 1 teaspoon vanilla extract)

Raspberry Coulis *(page 137)*

raspberries and blueberries, for garnish

1. Mix the gelatin and water in a small saucepan and let soften for 2 minutes. Heat over low until the gelatin is dissolved, about 1 minute. Remove from heat.

2. In a medium saucepan, add the cream, half and half, and sugar and bring to a boil over medium-high heat. Once just boiling, remove the pan from the heat and add the cream cheese, vanilla, and melted gelatin mixture. Split and scrape the seeds from the vanilla bean and add to the mixture. Mix well. Cool to room temperature.

3. Coat a ½ cup muffin tin (or any standard-size muffin tin or even 6 oz individual ramekins) with vegetable oil and fill eight of them evenly with the cream. Cover with plastic wrap and chill overnight, or at least 4 to 6 hours.

4. Run a sharp knife around the edge to loosen the suction. Carefully pop out onto plates drizzled with Raspberry Coulis *(page 137)* and garnish with fresh raspberries and blueberries.

Dana's Tip

Try flavoring the cream with different extracts and zests. You're only limited by your imagination. At the inn we served coconut-flavored panna cotta with lime zest and garnished it with kiwi and watermelon slices. But I've included a similar recipe for a coconut cream sauce for kiwi and watermelon in this cookbook (page 15). For cooler months I like to flavor with cinnamon, nutmeg, and clove and serve the spiced panna cotta in a pool of Maine maple syrup!

Roasted Plums *with* Thyme, Honey, *and* Vanilla Frozen Yogurt

The natural purple color when roasting the plums with the honey gives you an absolutely gorgeous and delicious clear sauce to drizzle on a white plate. It's both sweet and tart. They make a great accompaniment to Ginger Spice Pancakes *(page 49)* in the fall or winter. Roasting definitely enhances the color of this stone fruit. The sprinkle of fresh thyme just before serving looks lovely against the bright purple sauce.

Serves 4

2 tablespoons granulated sugar

3 tablespoons honey

4 firm purple plums

1 sprig fresh thyme

vanilla frozen yogurt (I love Gifford's French Vanilla — you'd swear it was ice cream!) or Fresh Whipped Cream *(page 142)*

I. Preheat the oven to 350 degrees.

2. Line a rimmed baking sheet with parchment paper a bit larger than the pan, to contain the juices.

3. Sprinkle the sugar on the parchment, then pour the honey onto the parchment.

4. Halve the plums and place cut-side down on the sugar and honey.

5. Sprinkle half of the thyme leaves onto the honey, and reserve the rest to garnish before serving.

6. Roast the plums for about 15 minutes, removing them from the oven just before they start to lose their shape or you see the skin wrinkle.

7. Place two halves in a bowl. Spoon some of the roasting liquid over the fruit. Add a scoop of vanilla frozen yogurt or top with whipped cream, and sprinkle with the rest of the thyme leaves.

Dana's Tip
Warm the honey for about 25 seconds in a glass cup in the microwave so it spreads once you pour it onto the parchment.

ROASTED PLUMS *with*
THYME, HONEY, *and*
VANILLA FROZEN YOGURT,
page 19

Cantaloupe *with* Green-Tea-Infused Minted Simple Syrup

This is a surprisingly fresh combination of fruit and herbs that's not overpowering. The fruit will soften after sitting in the syrup for a couple of days, so it is best eaten within twenty-four hours of the day it's made. *Serves 2 to 4*

1 fresh cantaloupe cut into small chunks
¼ cup Simple Syrup with Green Tea and Fresh Mint *(page 134)*
fresh mint, for garnish

I. Toss the cantaloupe with the syrup and refrigerate for a couple of hours or until nicely chilled. Garnish with a fresh mint leaf.

Dana's Tip
You'll end up with more waste when using a melon baller, but you could purée the scraps and make a smoothie or a chilled melon soup by adding sour cream.

Rum Raisin Pears

This makes a great winter fruit starter. Paired with a scoop of vanilla bean ice cream or frozen yogurt you can turn this breakfast fruit course into a lovely, decadent after-dinner treat, especially when served with a glass of Port wine. *Serves 4 to 6*

4 fairly firm Bosc pears

¹/₂ stick butter

¹/₂ cup light brown sugar

¹/₄ cup dark or spiced rum

¹/₄ cup raisins (I prefer gold, they seem softer)

¹/₄ cup heavy cream

dash of salt

a piece of cinnamon or star anise, for garnish

Fresh Whipped Cream *(page 142)*, for garnish

1. Peel, halve, and core the pears.

2. In a large sauté pan, add the butter and sugar and place the pears cut side down. Cook over medium heat for about 5 minutes. Add the rum and raisins and cook for another 3 minutes. Lower the heat, add the cream and salt and cook uncovered for another 3 to 4 minutes until the caramel turns golden.

3. Serve with garnishes and fresh whipped cream or a scoop of vanilla frozen yogurt.

Papaya, Mango, *and* Strawberries *with* Lemon *and* Basil

I learned about the combination of papaya and lemon in Mexico and have been hooked ever since. The lemon brings a welcome acidity to the papaya. I call this my Sunrise Maine Morning.

Serves 6 to 8

1 large ripe papaya, about 8 to 10 inches

3 ripe mangoes

1 pint of strawberries

1 cup Simple Syrup *(page 132)*

juice and zest of 3 large lemons

1. Peel and cut the papaya and mango into a medium dice. Make sure to remove the seeds from the papaya. Place the cut-up fruit in a large bowl. Roughly chop the strawberries and set aside in a small dish.

2. Add the Simple Syrup to the papaya and mango. Squeeze the juice from the lemons and add this to mixture. Add the zest from two of the lemons. Cover and refrigerate until well chilled.

3. Just before serving, toss in the strawberries and mix well.

4. Serve in cocktail or tall stemmed glasses. Add fresh zest from the remaining lemon over the top of each glass.

Dana's Tip
Strawberries will soften too quickly if placed in with the syrup with the other fruit.

Port Wine Poached Pears
with Vanilla Bean Crème

At the inn we served these pears chilled with a scoop of
Purple Basil Pear Sorbet *(page 31)*. This is a great do-ahead
dish, which makes it ideal for entertaining. Serving
them chilled is also refreshing during warmer summer
months. In the winter, opt for the warm Rum Raisin
Pears *(page 23)*. This is one dish that smells fabulous
during cooking. Since I made mine the day before
serving, it always happened that they were cooking
during check-in time. Not a bad aroma for guests to
enjoy.

Serves 4

4 firm Bosc pears

4 cups cranberry juice

1 cup granulated sugar

4 cups port wine

4 star anise pods

4 short cinnamon sticks (or 2 long sticks broken
  into pieces)

Vanilla Bean Crème *(page 141)*, **for garnish**

I. Peel, halve, and core the pears.

2. In a large saucepan, add the cranberry juice, sugar, port,
   star anise, and cinnamon and bring to boil. Add the
   pear halves, cover and lower heat to medium. Cook until
   tender, about 15 minutes. If the pears are soft, they'll
   need a few minutes less. Remove the pears and place cut-
   side down in a container. Allow the liquid to cool down
   quite a bit, then strain it and add to the pears and refrigerate at least 8 hours or
   overnight. Save the liquid for a batch of Purple Basil Pear Sorbet *(page 31)*.

3. Cut each pear half starting at one quarter inch from the stem end down to the
   bottom, at one-quarter-inch spacing and place on a plate, fanned.

4. Drizzle with the Vanilla Bean Crème and serve.

Dana's Tip

If you're serving the pears chilled, they will soften slightly in the poaching liquid overnight, so you may want to undercook them by a couple of minutes or judge your cooking time based on the pears you find. This might take practice – if they end up too soft, use them for a batch of Pear Sorbet. Also, using the star anise pods and cinnamon sticks as opposed to ground spices will keep your poaching liquid clear and not cloudy.

fruit course

Sorbets

Sorbets can be created from several ingredients, often easily improvised based on what's fresh, left over, or in your imagination. They can accompany a fruit dish, cleanse the palate between courses, or stand in for a light dessert. They're also a nice addition on a warm day or a great morning start in a smoothie on the run.

WATERMELON, LIME, *and*
COCONUT SORBET,
page 30

Watermelon, Lime, *and* Coconut Sorbet

This dish makes great use of leftover watermelon. I serve the sorbet in a piece of the watermelon rind and garnished with a couple of julienned strips of the rind. What a great frozen cocktail this would make! Maybe that'll be another cookbook.

Makes about 4 cups

5 cups cubed watermelon (about 1 small baby seedless)

1 cup coconut milk (well shaken)

juice and zest of 1 lime

1 teaspoon coconut extract

1 cup Simple Syrup *(page 132)*

¹/₂ cup honey

I. Purée the watermelon, coconut milk, lime juice and zest, coconut extract, Simple Syrup, and honey in a blender until smooth. Pour into plastic container, cover, and freeze for at least 12 to 14 hours.

2. When ready to serve, remove from the freezer for a few minutes, and use an ice cream scoop to mound into a dish, a stemmed glass, or a piece of the watermelon rind.

Raspberry Sorbet

This is classic simplicity. You could buy this at the market, but it's easy enough to make at home.

Makes about 4 cups

4 cups frozen raspberries, partially thawed (retain liquid)

juice of half a lemon

1 cup Simple Syrup *(page 132)*

I. Purée the raspberries, lemon juice, and Simple Syrup in a blender until smooth. Pour into plastic container, cover, and freeze for at least 12 to 14 hours.

2. When ready to serve, remove from freezer for a few minutes and use an ice cream scoop to mound into a stemmed glass or decorative bowl.

Purple Basil Pear Sorbet

This creation was a result of overripe pears that were just too soft after poaching for my Port Wine Poached Pears *(page 26)*. Add a simple syrup and freeze and you have a perfect summertime sorbet.

Makes about 3 cups

6 poached pears *(page 26)*
¹/₂ cup poaching liquid
¹/₂ cup Simple Syrup *(page 132)*
6 fresh basil leaves (purple if you can find it)
1 teaspoon ground cinnamon

I. Purée the pears, poaching liquid, Simple Syrup, basil, and cinnamon in a blender until smooth. Pour into plastic container, cover, and freeze for at least 12 to 14 hours.

2. When ready to serve, remove from freezer for a few minutes and use an ice cream scoop to mound into a stemmed glass or decorative bowl.

Papaya Mango Lemon Sorbet

Again, one of the beautiful things about a sorbet is the use of leftover fruit. I had papaya left over from my Sunrise Morning fruit dish and decided to make a sorbet. I added plenty of lemon and lemon zest for that refreshing zing! Add milk or yogurt and wheat germ, and you've got a breakfast smoothie on the run.

Makes about 5 cups

4 cups peeled, chopped, and seeded ripe mango and papaya
1 cup Simple Syrup *(page 132)*
juice from 3 lemons
zest from 1 lemon

I. Purée the mango, papaya, Simple Syrup, and lemon juice and zest in a blender until smooth. Pour into plastic container, cover, and freeze for at least 12 to 14 hours.

2. When ready to serve, remove from freezer for a few minutes and use an ice cream scoop to mound into a stemmed glass or decorative bowl.

CHAPTER 2

Sweet Entrées

Sweet Crepes

Whether you make them sweet or savory, the basic crepe recipe remains the same, with the exception of a small amount of sugar. I'll show you several variations of both sweet and savory to satisfy all taste buds. Crepes can be served folded and topped or stuffed and rolled. They can even be layered between ingredients. They're versatile, fun, and delicious.

Basic Sweet Crepes
Makes about 12 crepes (serves 6)

Batter

1⅓ cups milk (I use 2%)

4 large eggs

1⅓ cups flour

pinch of salt

1 tablespoon granulated sugar

½ stick butter, melted

I. Mix the milk, eggs, flour, salt, and sugar in a blender, scraping down the sides to incorporate all the ingredients. Slowly pour in the melted butter through the opening in the lid and mix for another few seconds. The consistency should be similar to heavy cream. Let the batter sit in the refrigerator at least 30 minutes or up to one day.

2. While the crepe batter rests, make the filling. Preheat the oven to 350 degrees.

Basic Cheese Filling
For 12 crepes

4 ounces softened cream cheese

½ pint cottage cheese (I use 4 percent)

1 pint ricotta cheese

½ cup granulated sugar

1 teaspoon vanilla extract

I. Place the cream, cottage, and ricotta cheeses in a food processor along with the sugar and vanilla extract and mix until very smooth.

2. Remove the crepe batter from the refrigerator. You'll need a shallow, non-stick frying

pan or crepe pan, 8 to 9 inches in diameter. Heat the pan over medium high heat. Coat with non-stick cooking spray or a little butter. Pour a small amount of batter (about ¼ cup) into the pan directly from the blender to coat the pan, swirling around to spread to ensure it stays thin. Cook until the edges just turn lightly brown, about 2 minutes, and flip to cook another 30 seconds or so. Remove the crepe by sliding it out of the pan to a piece of wax paper and repeat with the remaining batter, regreasing the pan each time and stacking crepes as they are done.

3. Place 2 tablespoons of filling in the center of each crepe. At this point, if you were adding ingredients, you'd do so now. Fold each side four times, creating small square pouches. Place the crepe seam side down onto a parchment-lined, rimmed baking sheet. Repeat with the remaining crepes.

4. Bake for 30 minutes until puffed. Dust the tops with powdered sugar and serve these basic cheese-filled crepes with any type of fresh fruit. I often use sliced strawberries that I let macerate (marinate) in 1 tablespoon of raspberry liqueur.

Pineapple, Cherry, *and* Pecan Cheese Crepes

This combination came about from leftover Pineapple Cherry Jam I made for the Popovers in this cookbook. The texture is very similar to a cranberry relish at Thanksgiving and would make a great alternative to one.

Makes about 12 crepes. Serves 6

Preheat the oven to 350 degrees.

1 batch **Basic Sweet Crepes** *(page 34)*, **batter and filling**
½ **cup Pineapple Cherry Jam** *(page 135)*
¼ **cup chopped pecans**

1. Mix the pecans with the jam.

2. Add 2 tablespoons of the basic cheese filing to the crepe and add 1 tablespoon of the jam/nut mixture on top. Fold each. Repeat with remaining crepes.

3. Cover the filled crepes with foil and bake for 30 minutes, until puffed, removing foil after 20 minutes. Dust the tops with powdered sugar, top with a small dollop of the jam/nut mixture, and enjoy!

Blueberry Apricot Cheese Crepes

Using the Basic Sweet Crepes from the previous page,
we'll add a few fruit components to flavor them.

Makes about 12 crepes (serves 6)

1 batch Basic Sweet Crepes *(page 34)*, **batter and filling**

¹/₂ **cup apricot preserves**

2 fresh apricots, chopped

1 tablespoon orange liqueur

1 pint fresh blueberries

1 fresh apricot, sliced, for garnish

I. In a small bowl, mix the preserves, chopped apricots, and liqueur. When filling the crepes, add 1 teaspoon preserve mixture and 1 tablespoon blueberries and fold. Move to baking sheet and repeat with the remainder of crepes.

2. Cover the filled crepes with foil and bake for 30 minutes, until puffed, removing foil after 20 minutes. Dust the tops with powdered sugar, top with fresh blueberries and apricot slices.

Cinnamon Baked Oatmeal Cake *with* Warm Rhubarb Sauce *and* Vanilla Bean Crème

This was one of the most surprising and requested recipes we served at the inn, probably because of its simplicity and the health benefits of oats. It was surprising as many people who don't typically like oatmeal really enjoyed this because of its cake-like texture. I even kept pre-printed cards with the inn's logo and recipe at the checkout desk in anticipation of the request! Give it a try: you just might convert some oatmeal naysayers like I did.

Serves 8 to 10

½ cup canola or vegetable oil

½ cup walnut oil

1¼ cups granulated sugar

4 large eggs

2 tablespoons ground cinnamon

2 teaspoons baking powder

1 teaspoon vanilla extract

1½ teaspoons salt

1 cup whole milk

1¼ cups half & half

6 cups thick-cut rolled oats (not quick cook or instant)

Vanilla Bean Crème *(page 141)*, for garnish

Rhubarb Sauce *(page 136)*, for garnish

sliced strawberries, for garnish

1. Combine the oils, sugar, eggs, cinnamon, baking powder, vanilla, salt, milk, and half & half in a mixer and beat until well combined. Add the oats and mix thoroughly.

2. Pour the mixture into a greased 9x13 glass baking dish, cover with plastic wrap, and chill in the refrigerator overnight.

3. Preheat the oven to 350 degrees. Remove the dish from refrigerator and allow it to sit while the oven is heating.

4. Bake uncovered for 30 minutes, until lightly brown on top. Cut into squares, place in shallow bowl, and top with the Vanilla Bean Crème and Rhubarb Sauce and garnish with some fresh sliced strawberries. This freezes and rewarms beautifully.

Chocolate, Banana, Raspberry French Toast

This was our signature sweet entrée at the inn. We'd alternate daily between sweet and savory, but this was often requested when the guests made their reservation. It's really a simple dish dressed with a couple of simple sauces, creating a symphony when combined.

Serves 4

3 large eggs

1 cup half & half

$1/4$ cup granulated sugar

$1/4$ teaspoon salt

$1/2$ teaspoon vanilla extract

3 ounces cream cheese, softened

8 slices thick-cut French toast bread

2 small ripe bananas

powdered sugar, for garnish

Raspberry Coulis *(page 137)*, for garnish

Dark Chocolate Sauce *(page 136)*, for garnish

fresh raspberries, for garnish

1. Preheat the oven to 325 degrees.

2. Combine the eggs, half & half, sugar, salt, and vanilla in blender and mix for about 5 seconds. Pour into a wide bowl for dipping.

3. Spread the softened cream cheese on one side of all eight slices of bread.

4. Thinly slice the bananas and divide among four slices of bread, layering evenly.

5. Place the top slice of bread on top of the layer of bananas, with the cream cheese side facing down. Dip each sandwich into the egg mixture to coat, making sure to soak thoroughly.

6. Fry on griddle or skillet over medium heat until browned on both sides, about 4 to 5 minutes per side.

7. Place on a parchment-lined sheet, cover with foil, and bake for 15 minutes until the center is heated through. Remove foil and cook another 3 minutes.

8. Remove from oven and let sit for 2 minutes before slicing on a diagonal. Dust with powdered sugar and serve with a drizzle of Raspberry Coulis *(page 137)*, Dark Chocolate Sauce *(page 136)*, accompanied by fresh raspberries and sliced bananas.

Lemon Zest French Toast
with Maine Blueberry Maple Syrup

This is a basic French toast recipe, but the lemon and blueberry is such a wonderful flavor combination. Again, opposite colors working beautifully. You could also use the Blackberry Coulis *(page 137)* with fresh blackberries instead.

Serves 4

3 large eggs

1 cup half & half

1/4 cup granulated sugar

1/4 teaspoon salt

1/2 teaspoon lemon extract

juice and zest of 1 lemon

8 slices thick–cut French toast bread

1 pint Maine blueberries

2 cups maple syrup

powdered sugar, for garnish

1. Combine eggs, half & half, sugar, salt, lemon extract, and lemon juice in blender and mix for about 4 to 5 seconds. Pour into a wide bowl for dipping.

2. Dip each slice of bread into the egg mixture and fry on a griddle over medium heat until browned on both sides, about 5 minutes.

3. Over low heat in a small saucepan, combine the blueberries with 2 cups of your favorite pure maple syrup, heat until warm.

4. To plate, diagonally cut each slice of French toast, layering four pieces across each plate. Dust with powdered sugar, lemon zest (one pass over the zester), top with 2 to 3 tablespoons of the warm blueberry maple syrup.

Monte Cristo *with* Ham, Maine Maple Mustard, Pears, *and* Havarti

This was a dish inspired by a famous French-style creperie restaurant near my hometown of Bethesda, Maryland. They had a wonderful fried Monte Cristo. This is my griddled version for breakfast. It satisfies guests with a sweet or savory preference.

Serves 4

4 large eggs

1 cup half & half

1/4 teaspoon salt

1/4 cup sweet brown mustard

1/2 cup plus 2 tablespoons Maine maple syrup

8 slices of Challah or other thick-cut egg bread

16 slices of thinly sliced smoked ham

8 slices of Havarti (or Monterey Jack)

1 ripe but firm Bosc pear, sliced

fresh raspberries, for garnish

raspberry preserves, for garnish

1. Preheat the oven to 325 degrees.

2. Mix the eggs, half & half, mustard, 2 tablespoons of the maple syrup, and salt in blender for 5 seconds and pour into a wide bowl for dipping.

3. Layer four slices of the bread with cheese, ham, sliced pear, and another layer of cheese, then top with the remaining 4 slices of bread. Cut in half. Dip the sandwich halves into the egg mixture and fry on a griddle over medium heat until brown on both sides, about 5 minutes. Move the sandwiches to a parchment-lined cookie sheet when done. Cover and place the cookie sheet in oven for 20 minutes, uncovering after 15, until completely heated through.

4. Serve the two halves on a plate with fresh raspberries, maple syrup, and a small ramekin of raspberry preserves. (Sometimes I add diced kiwi for color and a light acidic bite.)

Dana's Tip
I buy Hannaford Inspirations brand "Maine Maple Mustard,"
which is absolutely delicious, if you can find it.

MONTE CRISTO *with*
HAM, MAINE MAPLE
MUSTARD, PEARS,
and HAVARTI,
page 41

Cheese Blintz Soufflé *with* Mango Puree, Blackberry Coulis, *and* Local Maine Blackberries

This dish combines the flavor and ingredients of a cheese-filled blintz or crepe, but in a baked souffle form. It was a dish inspired by one of my favorite brunch recipes made with store-bought blintzes that my mother and cousin would make for family gatherings or holidays. I decided to use our local Maine blackberries because they seem sweeter and less tart than the mass-produced variety. Add Blackberry Coulis *(page 137)* and Mango Puree *(page 140)* and you have delicious art on a plate. Guests would come into the kitchen while I was "painting" with my sauces and get such a kick out of me! Sometimes I'd do every plate with a different design.

Serves 8

Filling

¹/₃ cup granulated sugar

1 egg yolk

1 cup cottage cheese (I use 4 percent, but you can use 1 percent)

8 ounces softened cream cheese

1 tablespoon vanilla extract

Batter

1¹/₂ sticks unsalted butter, softened

1¹/₂ cups sour cream

³/₄ cup granulated sugar

5 eggs

1³/₄ cups plus 1 tablespoon flour

5 teaspoons baking powder

2 tablespoons milk (2 percent or whole)

¹/₂ cup orange juice (low or no pulp)

Garnish

Mango Puree *(page 140)*

Blackberry Coulis *(page 137)*

fresh blackberries

powdered sugar

1. Preheat the oven to 350 degrees.

2. In a food processor, mix the sugar, egg yolk, cottage cheese, cream cheese, and vanilla and set aside.

3. To make the batter, in a stand mixer, add the butter, sour cream, and sugar and combine until smooth. Add the eggs one at a time while mixing and blend again until smooth. Add the flour and baking powder and mix on low while adding the milk and orange juice. Blend until just mixed, though the batter may remain slightly lumpy.

4. Liberally coat a 9x12 glass baking dish with butter or vegetable oil. Layer half of the batter on the bottom. Carefully dollop the filling over the batter, keeping it at least a half inch from the edges. Top the filling with the remaining batter.

5. Bake uncovered for 45 minutes, until lightly browned. Cover and lower the heat to 275 degrees for another 10 minutes. Remove from oven and allow to rest for 5 to 10 minutes before cutting. This allows the filling to set and not fall apart when slicing. (I learned the hard way!)

6. Serve with Mango Puree *(page 140)*, Blackberry Coulis *(page 137)*, and fresh blackberries and dust with powdered sugar.

45

Dana's Tip

The batter and filling for this can be made a day ahead and stored
in the refrigerator. Make sure you use double-acting baking powder.
And let it sit at room temperature for about 30 minutes before
assembling and placing in the oven to bake.

Blueberry Oatmeal Streusel
French Toast *with* Warm Maple Rum Sauce

There are thousands of baked French toast recipes out there; with this one I've created bread pudding meets baked French toast meets egg custard. The crunchy pecan streusel topping is addictive. But then so is the rum sauce. I used to walk into the dining room at the inn with my squeeze bottle to offer more. Seriously! Fresh sliced peaches make a nice accompaniment to this dish.

Serves 8 to 10

1 cup chopped pecans

12 slices thick-cut bread

1 pint blueberries

8 large eggs

3 cups half & half

¼ cup light brown sugar

1 tablespoon vanilla extract

1 tablespoon ground cinnamon

1 stick unsalted butter, softened

1 cup packed light brown sugar

2 tablespoons dark corn syrup

1 cup thick rolled oats (not instant or quick cooking)

¼ teaspoon ground nutmeg (less if fresh grated)

Maple-Rum Sauce *(page 135)*, **for garnish**

fresh peaches, sliced, for garnish

fresh blueberries, for garnish

1. Preheat the oven to 350 degrees. Coat a 9x12 glass baking dish with butter or vegetable oil.

2. Toast the pecans in a single layer on rimmed baking sheet in the oven for 15 minutes. Set aside.

3. Cut the bread into 1-inch cubes and layer evenly in baking dish. Sprinkle blueberries on top.

4. Combine the eggs, half & half, sugar, vanilla, and cinnamon in a blender for about 5 seconds. (If mixing in a stand mixer, beat for 2 minutes on medium-high.) Pour the mixture over bread.

5. For the topping, combine the butter, sugar, and corn syrup in a mixing bowl outfitted with a paddle and mix on medium-high until creamy, about 2 minutes. Fold in the toasted pecans, oats, and nutmeg and mix just to combine.

6. Dollop and carefully spread the topping onto the top of the bread. Cover with foil and refrigerate overnight.

7. Bring the dish to room temperature before baking. When ready to bake, preheat the oven to 375 degrees.

8. Place the dish over a rimmed baking sheet as this will drip when baking (oven fires are not a good thing, learn from my mishaps!).

9. Bake covered in foil for about 40 minutes. Remove the foil and bake for another 10 minutes. Reduce the oven to 275 degrees and let sit in oven for another 10 minutes.

10. Remove from oven and let rest for 10 minutes before slicing (very important to let it rest before slicing or it will not hold its shape). Slice down the middle of the pan, then into 4 or 5 slices across.

11. Drizzle the warm Maple-Rum Sauce *(page 135)* over the top of each slice and serve with fresh sliced peaches and blueberries.

Dana's Tip

In addition to being an easy make-ahead dish, this freezes and rewarms beautifully if you send your friends and family home with leftovers.

Classic Malted Belgian Waffles *with* Grand Marnier Maple Syrup, Toasted Coconut, Toasted Macadamias, *and* Fresh Whipped Cream

Makes 12 four-inch Belgian-style waffles

2 ¼ cups flour

2 tablespoons granulated sugar

⅛ teaspoon salt

½ cup canola or vegetable oil

1½ cups 2 percent milk

1 egg

¼ cup malted milk powder

2 tablespoons baking powder

1½ cups maple syrup

2 tablespoons Grand Marnier

juice from 1 orange

toasted shredded coconut, for garnish

toasted chopped macadamias, for garnish

zest of 1 orange, for garnish

Fresh Whipped Cream *(page 142)*, for garnish

1. In a large bowl, combine the flour, sugar, salt, oil, milk, egg, malted milk powder, and baking powder and mix with a whisk until well combined.

2. Heat a waffle iron and coat with cooking spray. Ladle the batter into the iron and cook until golden brown, about 8 minutes.

3. While waffles are cooking, spread the coconut and macadamia nuts on a sheet pan lined with parchment and toast in oven at 300 degrees until very lightly browned.

4. In a small pot, combine the syrup, Grand Marnier, and orange juice, and stir until heated through.

5. Serve with orange maple syrup and toppings for garnish.

Dana's Tip
To make pancakes using this recipe, just add 1 more egg and ¼ cup less milk. Classic Maine Blueberry Pancakes! Or for Ginger Spice Pancakes, add ¼ teaspoon nutmeg, ¼ teaspoon ginger (fresh if available), and ½ teaspoon cinnamon.

Fluffy Chocolate Ricotta Pancakes

This dish is one inspired by my favorite chocolate ricotta-filled Italian cannolis with my own citrus twist. When my eleven-year-old niece, Lauren, learned I was writing a cookbook, she wanted me to include a recipe for a pancake taco: "Aunt Dana, it's a pancake folded in half filled with whipped cream and strawberries!" I told her that it sounded fun and delicious, but that I already had a pancake recipe for the book!

Serves 4

1 cup ricotta cheese

1 cup lowfat milk

1 tablespoon extra virgin olive oil

1/2 teaspoon orange extract

3 eggs, separated

3 tablespoons granulated sugar

1 tablespoon cocoa powder

1/4 teaspoon salt

1 tablespoon baking powder

1 1/2 cups flour

2 cups maple syrup

juice from 2 oranges

1 tablespoon Grand Marnier

powdered sugar, for garnish

orange slices and zest, for garnish

1/4 cup mini chocolate chips, for garnish (optional)

1. In a mixer, blend the ricotta cheese, milk, olive oil, orange extract, egg yolks, and sugar until smooth. Add the cocoa powder, 1/8 teaspoon of the salt, the baking powder, and flour and blend.

2. In a separate bowl, whisk the egg whites with the remaining 1/8 teaspoon of salt and beat until stiff.

3. Add the egg whites to the batter, folding gently to incorporate. Drop the batter onto a hot griddle, flipping when they just begin to bubble. Meanwhile, combine the maple syrup, orange juice, and Grand Marnier in a small bowl. Dust the finished pancakes with powdered sugar and serve with the orange maple syrup and fresh orange slices. Zest some orange peel on top before serving. Add the mini chocolate chips for the chocoholic!

Maine Blueberry Malted Belgian Waffles
with **Maple Syrup** *and* **Fresh Whipped Cream**

There's just something about the flavor of a blueberry waffle served with buttery, pure maple syrup. Simple and delicious!

Makes 12 waffles

2¼ cups flour

2 tablespoons granulated sugar

⅛ teaspoon salt

½ cup canola or vegetable oil

1½ cups 2 percent milk

1 egg

¼ cup malted milk powder

2 tablespoons baking powder

1 cup Maine blueberries (thaw and drain well if you use frozen berries)

Fresh Whipped Cream *(page 142)*, for garnish

I. In a large bowl, combine the flour, sugar, salt, oil, milk, egg, malted milk powder, and baking powder and mix with a whisk until well combined. Do not over mix—it's OK if the batter is slightly lumpy. Gently fold in the blueberries, using caution not to break them.

2. Heat a waffle iron and liberally coat it with cooking spray.

3. Ladle the batter onto waffle iron and cook until golden brown, about 8 minutes. To keep the waffles warm and crisp, keep them covered in a 250-degree oven and then just before serving uncover to expose waffles to the dry heat for a few minutes, then plate.

Dana's Tip

Malted milk powder can be purchased at specialty baking stores or online. Ovaltine is not the equivalent, as it has added ingredients. I like The Bakers Catalog for a variety of baking supplies. Also, invest in a good quality Belgian waffle iron—the highest wattage you can find. It makes a big difference in how quickly the waffles cook and how well they crisp up. I think the malt powder might have something to do with the crisp factor, too.

CHAPTER 3

Savory Entrées

Fried Eggs on Wild Mushroom Hash *with* Melted Swiss

This dish really can't get much easier or fresher. It's gluten-free and still filling.

Serves 4

2 tablespoons extra virgin olive oil

4 tablespoons unsalted butter

4 cups of a variety of mushrooms — (Shiitake, Chanterelles, Morels are my favorites), roughly chopped

1 large bunch scallions (trimmed 1 inch from top and bottom), using both white and green parts, sliced 1/8 – 1/4 inch thick

2 cups shredded Swiss cheese (you could substitute sharp cheddar or Monterey Jack)

8 eggs

1/2 teaspoon paprika

salt, to taste

freshly ground black pepper, to taste

I. Preheat the oven to warm, about 175 to 190 degrees.

2. In a large sauté pan over medium heat, add the olive oil and 3 tablespoons of the butter to the pan. Add the mushrooms and half of the scallions and sauté until soft, about 10 minutes. Add the remaining scallions and top with the cheese. Cover and lower heat to a very low simmer for 5 minutes. Remove and place in warm oven until ready to plate.

3. Using a 12- to 14-inch frying pan, add the remaining 1 tablespoon of butter. When melted, crack the eggs one at a time into the pan and fry each to the desired level of doneness. Keep in warm oven, covered, until all eggs are cooked. If you don't have a large frying pan, use two smaller ones and cook the eggs 4 in each pan.

4. Divide the mushroom mixture among plates, top each with two fried eggs, sprinkle with paprika, salt, and pepper.

Egg Roulade Filled *with* Sautéed Leeks *and* Parmesan, Topped *with* Lobster, Sherry, *and* Melted Butter

Roulade simply means "rolled". This is constructed just like a jelly roll on a sheet pan, but with egg; it's basically a rolled and baked omelet. The results are worth the extra steps. This version was our signature savory dish at the inn, a particular favorite for the chunks of fresh Maine lobster on top. This is one of the most indulgent entrées we served, but it was worth every calorie and penny. We even received a recipe request from *Gourmet* Magazine, but unfortunately, our recipe didn't make it into the magazine before we sadly had to say farewell to the publication. So here it is.

Serves 4 to 6

8 eggs

2 cups plus 2 tablespoons heavy cream

1 teaspoon salt

2 tablespoons extra virgin olive oil

3 large leeks, washed and thinly sliced

one (8-ounce) package cream cheese

1 teaspoon Worcestershire sauce

juice from 1/4 lemon

1 stick plus 3 tablespoons butter

1 1/2 cups shredded Parmesan cheese

1/2 cup dry sherry

16 ounces fresh, cooked lobster meat, cut into small chunks

one (10-ounce) package baby spinach, washed and dried

fresh chopped chives, for garnish

I. Preheat the oven to 350 degrees.

2. Grease a rimmed heavy-duty half sheet pan with butter or vegetable oil, then line with parchment paper, and then grease the parchment, making sure to press it flat to the surface of the pan, leaving at least an inch overhang.

3. In a blender, mix the eggs, 2 cups of cream, and $1/2$ teaspoon salt on high speed for 4 to 5 seconds. Pour the mixture into the lined baking sheet. Bake until you begin to see the surface of the egg just start to brown, about 20 minutes. Remove and let cool.

4. While cooling, heat the olive oil in a pan over medium–high heat. Sauté the leeks, covered, until soft, about 10 to 12 minutes. When soft, add the cream cheese, Worcestershire sauce, the remaining 2 tablespoons of cream, lemon juice, and the remaining $1/2$ teaspoon of salt and stir. When the cream cheese is thoroughly incorporated, add three tablespoons of butter, mix in, and remove from heat. Let cool for about 3 minutes.

5. Dollop small amounts of the leek filling onto the egg. Using an offset spatula, carefully spread the mixture over the entire egg sponge, trying not to tear the egg as it is very delicate. Sprinkle the Parmesan over the filling.

6. Here's the fun part: the rolling. With the short edge of the pan closest to you using the parchment as a guide, roll the egg up onto itself (like a Hostess Ho-Ho!) until you end up with the egg seam on the underside of the roll. Keep the egg covered with the parchment left after rolling as it will help keep the egg moist. Cover the entire roll with aluminum foil and bake for another 20 minutes.

7. While baking, melt the remaining stick of butter in a pan with the sherry and cook for about 5 minutes, allowing much of the alcohol to burn off. Then add the lobster, lower the heat, and cover. Simmer for 5 minutes.

8. To serve, place a pile of fresh baby spinach on a plate. Slice the roulade into 4 to 6 slices, layer onto the spinach, and top with a couple of spoonfuls of the lobster butter. Garnish with fresh chives.

Dana's Tip
The size of the pan is imperative to the successful rolling of the egg, believe me,
I tried several pan sizes and ratios of eggs to cream. This is it.

Bacon, Onion, Tomato, *and* Smoked Cheddar Roulade

This Roulade is filled with sautéed bacon, onion, and tomato and topped with shredded smoked cheddar and regular sharp cheddar. Other variations might include layering pesto and herbed cheese with Parmesan, sun-dried tomatoes, or any vegetables. Just be sure to sauté your vegetables first so that the moisture doesn't come out in the Roulade during the second baking.

Serves 4 to 6

8 eggs

2 cups plus 2 tablespoons heavy cream

1 teaspoon salt

4 Roma or Italian tomatoes

3 tablespoons extra virgin olive oil

1 teaspoon granulated garlic

6 strips thick cut bacon

1 large yellow onion

4 ounces grated smoked cheddar

4 ounces sharp cheddar

baby mixed salad greens

I. Preheat the oven to 350 degrees.

2. Grease a rimmed heavy-duty half sheet pan (18x13) with butter or vegetable oil, then line with parchment paper, and then grease the parchment, making sure to press it flat to the surface of the pan, leaving at least an inch overhang.

3. In blender, mix the eggs, 2 cups of cream, and ½ teaspoon salt on high speed for 4 to 5 seconds. Pour the mixture into the lined baking sheet. Bake until you begin to see the surface of the egg just start to brown, about 20 minutes. Remove and set aside to cool.

4. Increase oven temperature to 400 degrees.

5. Chop the tomatoes into medium dice and toss with olive oil, salt, and garlic. Place on a parchment-lined baking sheet and roast for 30 minutes.

6. Meanwhile, chop the bacon and sauté until crisp and brown. Remove from bacon grease and set into small bowl. Chop the onion into small dice and add to the bacon

grease. Sauté over medium heat until lightly browned, about 10 to 13 minutes. Let the onions and tomatoes cool for about 10 minutes.

7. Evenly spread the tomatoes, onions, and ¾ of the bacon over the egg. Sprinkle the cheese and freshly ground black pepper to taste.

8. With the short edge of the pan closest to you, using the parchment as a guide, roll the egg up onto itself (like a Hostess Ho-Ho!), until you end up with the egg seam on the underside of the roll. Keep the egg covered with the parchment left after rolling as it will help keep the egg moist. Cover the entire roll with aluminum foil and bake for another 20 minutes.

9. Slice into 4 to 6 slices and serve atop the bed of baby salad greens. Garnish with the remaining bacon.

Open-Face Oefs Croque Monsieur (Ham *and* Cheese *with* Eggs)

Sometimes the most successful breakfast entrées are the ones with the simplest ingredients. This is a beautifully delicious example of that. It's a twist on the classic French ham and cheese sandwich with the addition of eggs.

Serves 4

8 slices thick-cut French or sourdough bread, both sides buttered (one slice large enough to hold two eggs or two smaller slices per person)

Dijon mustard

16 thin slices Smoked Black Forest or Virginia Baked Ham

8 slices ripe heirloom or beefsteak tomato

1 cup shredded Parmesan cheese

1 cup shredded Swiss cheese

freshly ground black pepper, to taste

1 tablespoon unsalted butter

8 eggs

salt, to taste

I. Preheat the oven to 375 degrees.

2. Lightly brown the buttered slice of bread in a sauté pan. Remove from the pan and spread a small amount of Dijon mustard on each slice. Place mustard side up onto a rimmed baking sheet lined with parchment paper and add 1 tablespoon each of shredded Swiss and Parmesan cheese, 2 slices of ham, 1 slice of tomato, and a few cracks of pepper. Top with 2 more tablespoons of cheese and some more pepper. (I'm liberal with the cheese, so feel free to be as well.)

3. Place in the oven until the cheese is melted and begins to bubble, about 10 minutes. While waiting, heat the butter in a pan and gently crack the eggs and cook sunny side up. When the egg is cooked to your liking, remove the bread from the oven and plate with two cooked eggs on top. Add a dash of salt and more pepper and enjoy!

Italian Baked Eggs *in* Roasted Tomato Sauce *with* Fennel

The homemade roasted tomato sauce is worth the extra step in this dish. Good quality Parmesan and fresh Buffalo mozzarella are important as well.

Serves 4

1 large fennel bulb, cored, trimmed, and chopped into a small (1-inch) dice

3 small onions, 2 quartered and 1 diced

1/4 cup extra virgin olive oil

12 medium-size ripe tomatoes, halved

1/2 teaspoon salt

1 teaspoon sugar

1/4 teaspoon dried red pepper flakes

8 eggs

8 ounces shredded mozzarella cheese

1/2 cup shredded Parmesan cheese

1. Preheat the oven to 375 degrees.

2. Toss the fennel cubes and the diced onion with half of the 1/4 cup of olive oil and roast until caramelized, about 40 minutes. Cover with foil and cook for another 20 minutes until soft.

3. In the same oven on a separate sheet pan, roast the tomatoes and the 2 quartered onions with the remaining olive oil in the oven for about 45 minutes until caramelized. Add the salt, sugar, and red pepper and purée with an immersion blender (or in blender, using caution when blending hot liquid).

4. Divide the roasted fennel and onion evenly among four gratin or individual baking dishes (deeper ones work better and tend not to allow the egg to dry out). Divide the tomato sauce evenly among each baking dish. Crack two eggs into each dish, and top with fresh mozzarella and Parmesan. Bake for 25 minutes, or until the eggs are cooked to your liking.

,

Chive *and* Cream Cheese Scrambled Eggs *in* Wonton Cups

This is a fun and delightful way to serve simple scrambled eggs. Add salsa, cheddar, and some crumbled spicy sausage and you have a nice Latin-inspired breakfast.

Serves 4

16 wonton wrappers

12 large eggs

1 cup heavy cream

1 bunch scallions, trimmed 1 inch from top and bottom, using both white and green parts, sliced ⅛ to ¼ inch thick

one (8-ounce) package cream cheese

¼ teaspoon salt

freshly ground black pepper

64

1. Preheat the oven to 350 degrees.

2. Coat a popover pan with non-stick cooking spray. Take 3 to 4 wonton wrappers for each popover cavity and line it, overlapping the wrappers. Be sure to get a wrapper into the bottom.

3. Bake until the tops are lightly browned, about 15 minutes. Then cover carefully with foil and bake another 15 minutes. This allows the wonton wrappers inside the pan to continue browning without over-browning the edges. Let the wrappers sit to cool a few minutes and place each on individual serving plates.

4. Mix the eggs and the cream in blender for 5 seconds.

5. Coat a large frying pan with non-stick cooking spray. Over medium heat, pour the eggs and scallions into pan and slowly cook until eggs are almost scrambled.

6. Add the cream cheese in small dollops and continue to cook until the eggs are set, just another minute or so. Add salt and pepper to taste

7. To serve, portion ¼ of the eggs in each wonton cup. You could serve this version with salsa on the side and a few slices of ripe avocado and fresh heirloom tomatoes.

Dana's Tip

Popover pans are designed specifically with a lip that forces the popover up and out to expand, creating the signature balloon shaped top. The pan works perfectly in this recipe since it's tall and holds the wonton wrappers in place vertically.

Asparagus, Caramelized Shallots, *and* Goat Cheese Frittata

This recipe holds up well in a warm oven for an extended period of time, likely due to the heavy cream. I don't incorporate my toppings into the frittata, in case an item is not to someone's taste, it can be removed without ruining the whole dish for them. I use Fiddleheads when they're in season in Maine during a few weeks in early spring.

Fiddleheads are the unfurled fronds of a fern and several varieties are harvested; cinnamon ferns are one of them. I think they are similar in taste and texture to asparagus and broccolini.

Serves 6 to 8

20 large eggs

1 ³/₄ cups heavy cream

1 teaspoon salt

freshly ground black pepper

4 shallots, diced

2 tablespoons extra virgin olive oil

1 ¹/₂ to 2 cups asparagus, cut into 1-inch pieces

4 ounces goat cheese

I. Mix the eggs, cream, and salt in blender for about 4 to 5 seconds. (A blender really incorporates air and increases the volume dramatically.)

2. Preheat the oven to 325 degrees.

3. In a small skillet over low-medium heat, add the olive oil and sauté the shallots until caramelized, about 16 to 18 minutes.

4. Steam the asparagus in the microwave in a bowl covered with a wet paper towel for 2 minutes. (If using fiddleheads, boil the fiddleheads until tender, about 15 minutes, and drain.)

5. Heat an ovenproof 10-inch non-stick skillet over medium-high heat. Add the egg mixture and stir constantly with a heatproof rubber spatula until curds form. Once you see curds form, quickly lower the heat and continue to move the eggs around, never stopping, almost as if to scramble. Remove from heat when the eggs are about half set. This helps the bottom from cooking in place and browning.

6. Place on the center rack in oven for about 10 minutes.

7. Remove from oven and top with the goat cheese, shallots, and asparagus. Finish in the oven for another 10 minutes, just until the toppings warm slightly.

8. Let sit 3 to 4 minutes before slicing and serving.

Frittata *with* Smoked Salmon, Sunset Acres Goat Cheese, Red Onion, Capers, Fresh Scallions, *and* Fresh Dill

There are several smokehouses in Maine that produce some of the best smoked salmon I've tasted; Ducktrap and Sullivan Harbor are two wonderful producers. Be sure to buy cold-smoked salmon and not the hot-smoked variety: the salmon smoked at a very low temperature tends to look, feel, and taste more like sushi, but with the smoke flavor. Cold smoked is what's traditionally used with bagels and cream cheese.

Serves 6 to 8

20 large eggs

1 3/4 cups heavy cream

1 teaspoon salt

freshly ground black pepper

4 ounces smoked salmon, chopped

4 ounces crumbled goat cheese

1/4 red onion, diced

3 stalks scallions, trimmed 1 inch from top and bottom, using both white and green parts, sliced 1/8 to 1/4 inch thick

1 tablespoon capers

1 tablespoon chopped fresh dill

1 tablespoon chopped fresh parsley

one (10-ounce) bag baby spinach

1 lemon, for garnish

I. Preheat the oven to 325 degrees.

2. Mix the eggs, cream, salt, and pepper in blender for 4 to 5 seconds.

3. Heat an ovenproof 10-inch non-stick skillet over medium-high heat. Add the egg mixture and stir constantly with a heatproof rubber spatula until curds form. Once you see curds form quickly, lower the heat, continue to move the eggs around, never stopping, almost as if to scramble. Remove from heat when the eggs are about half set. This helps the bottom from cooking in place and browning.

4. Place in oven for 20 minutes until set. Remove from oven and top with the salmon, goat cheese, onion, scallions, capers, dill, and parsley. The cool toppings offer a nice contrast to warm egg. Slice the frittata into 6 to 8 portions and serve over baby spinach with a fresh lemon wedge.

Savory Crepes

These are a few of my favorite things…for breakfast, brunch, lunch, or a light dinner paired with a salad and glass of white wine or bubbly. *Makes 12 crepes (serves 6)*

Basic Savory Crepes

1¹/₃ cups milk (I use 2 percent)

4 large eggs

1¹/₃ cups flour

pinch of salt

¹/₂ stick butter, melted

1. Mix the milk, eggs, flour, and salt in a blender, scraping down the sides to incorporate all the ingredients. Pour the melted butter through the opening in the lid and mix for another few seconds. Let the batter sit in the refrigerator at least 30 minutes or up to one day.

2. Remove the batter from refrigerator. You'll need a shallow non-stick frying pan or crepe pan, 8 to 9 inches in diameter. Heat over medium-high heat. Coat with non-stick cooking spray or butter. Add a small amount to coat the pan, swirling the batter around to spread to ensure it stays thin. Heat until the edges just turn brown, about 2 minutes, and flip to cook for another 30 seconds or so. Remove to piece of wax paper and repeat with remaining batter, stacking the crepes.

Ricotta, Butternut Squash, *and* Zucchini Crepes *with* Sage Brown Butter

I love the combination of savory and sweet in this crepe. The sweetness of the caramelized onions and the sweet squash puree are a lovely combination.

1 batch Basic Savory Crepes *(page 69)*

1 whole butternut squash

2 sweet onions

1 medium zucchini

1 tablespoon extra virgin olive oil

15 ounces ricotta cheese

1 cup cottage cheese

1 egg yolk

1/2 teaspoon salt

1 stick butter

2 large sage leaves

freshly ground black pepper

1. Preheat the oven to 350 degrees.

2. Halve and seed the squash and roast until soft, about 45 to 55 minutes. Once cooled slightly, remove the skin.

3. While the squash is roasting, slice the onions and dice the zucchini and sauté in olive oil until lightly browned and soft, about 10 to 12 minutes.

4. Put the squash, ricotta, cottage cheese, egg yolk, and salt in food processor and mix until very smooth.

5. Place 2 tablespoons of the filling in the center of each crepe. Add 1 tablespoon of the zucchini and onion mixture and fold in each side, creating small square pouches. Place seam side down onto a parchment-lined, rimmed baking sheet. Repeat with the remaining crepes. Cover and bake the crepes for 20 minutes until puffed. Uncover and cook for another 5 minutes.

6. Heat the butter in a small sauté pan over low heat with sage leaves until the butter just starts to brown, about 10 minutes (it will first bubble, then brown). Remove the sage leaves.

7. To serve, place two crepes on a plate and drizzle with the browned butter. Add freshly cracked black pepper to taste.

Asparagus, Parmesan, *and* Ricotta Crepes *with* Fresh Maine Crab *and* Browned Butter

This is my version of Crepes Oscar and a delicious way to enjoy Maine crab in its simplest form, without overpowering the delicate flavor of the crab.

1 batch Basic Savory Crepes *(page 69)*

18 stems of asparagus, cut in half

15 ounces ricotta cheese

1 cup cottage cheese

1 egg yolk

1/2 teaspoon salt

1 cup grated Parmesan cheese

1/2 cup shredded Parmesan cheese

1 stick butter

8 ounces fresh, cooked crab meat

lemon, for garnish

1. Preheat the oven to 350 degrees.

2. Steam the asparagus in a microwave for 2 minutes.

3. Put the ricotta, cottage cheese, egg yolk, salt, and grated Parmesan in a food processor and mix until very smooth.

4. Place 2 tablespoons of filling in the center of each crepe. Add 3 pieces of asparagus and 1 tablespoon shredded Parmesan and fold in each side, creating small rectangular pouches. Place seam side down onto a parchment-lined, rimmed baking sheet. Repeat with remaining crepes.

5. Cover and bake for 20 minutes until puffed. Uncover and bake 5 minutes.

6. Heat the butter in a small sauté pan over low heat until it just starts to brown, about 10 minutes.

7. Add the crab meat and stir to warm, 2 minutes. Turn off the heat and cover until ready to use.

8. To serve, place two crepes on a plate, top with the crab meat, and drizzle with the browned butter (about 2 tablespoons) and a squeeze of lemon.

ASPARAGUS, PARMESAN,
and RICOTTA CREPES *with*
FRESH MAINE CRAB *and*
BROWNED BUTTER,
page 71

Poached Eggs *on* Potato, Onion, *and* Bacon Hash *with* Grated Sharp White Cheddar, Truffled Sour Cream, *and* Fresh Chives

This is my breakfast version of a loaded baked potato! Delicious as a brunch or light dinner as well.

Serves 4

1 cup sour cream

1 teaspoon white truffle oil (I use Fiore)

1/2 teaspoon salt

1 tablespoon fresh chopped chives, plus more for garnish

4 strips thick-cut (hardwood smoked) bacon, diced

2 tablespoons extra virgin olive oil

1 large Vidalia (or sweet) onion, diced

2 large Yukon Gold potatoes, cubed

1/2 teaspoon paprika

1 cup shredded sharp white cheddar cheese

1/4 cup white vinegar

8 eggs

one (10-ounce) package of fresh baby spinach

1. Preheat the oven to 250 degrees.

2. In a small bowl, mix together the sour cream, truffle oil, salt, and chives and set aside.

3. In a large sauté pan, cook the bacon over medium heat until crisp, about 10 to 12 minutes, and remove with a slotted spoon. Set aside. To the same pan add the olive oil and sauté the onions and potatoes until tender and the onions are lightly caramelized, about 15 to 18 minutes. Add the paprika, toss in the bacon, top with shredded cheddar, and keep covered in the oven.

4. Fill a shallow sauté pan (2 to 3 quarts) 3/4 the way up with water and add the white vinegar. Bring to a slow rolling boil.

5. Crack one egg into a small bowl and lower into the boiling water. Repeat with the next

7 eggs. Cook for 3 to 4 minutes for a softer yolk. Remove the eggs and place in bowl of warm water to keep warm.

6. When ready to serve, remove the eggs from the warm water with a slotted spoon and place on a paper towel. To plate, put a small amount of baby spinach on each plate. Top with the potato hash, 2 poached eggs, and a tablespoon or two of the sour cream mixture. Garnish with fresh chopped chives.

Dana's Tip

In this section I've included some wonderful gluten-free options to the standard Eggs Benedict. During my time as an innkeeper I learned just how common intolerance to gluten was, and I tried to work my breakfasts around our guests' needs. With a few key ingredients, you've got a wonderful breakfast for everyone.

Poached Eggs *on a* Sweet Potato Pancake Topped *with* Creamed Caramelized Shallots *and* Poblano Peppers

The combination of the sweet potatoes with the slightly spicy cream sauce is just perfect. You'll never miss the English muffin or the Hollandaise.

Serves 6

2 tablespoons extra virgin olive oil

4 large shallots, diced

1 large Poblano pepper, seeds and ribs removed and cut into a very small dice

1 pint sour cream

3 tablespoons heavy cream

salt

freshly ground black pepper

1/4 cup white vinegar

12 extra-large eggs

3 tablespoons fresh chopped chives

one (10-ounce) package of fresh baby spinach

Sweet Potato Pancakes *(page 125)*

I. In a separate pan with the olive oil, sauté the shallots and pepper until softened and lightly caramelized, about 8 to 10 minutes. Remove from heat. Add the sour cream, heavy cream, salt, and pepper to taste. Set aside, covered.

2. In a shallow sauté pan (2 to 3 quarts), fill 3/4 with water and add the white vinegar. Bring to a slow rolling boil.

3. While shallots and peppers are cooking, crack one egg into a small bowl and lower into the boiling water. Repeat with the next 5 eggs. Cook 3 to 4 minutes (if you like a soft, runny yolk). Remove and place into a bowl of warm water to keep warm. Then cook the remaining 6 eggs.

4. Remove the eggs from warm water with a slotted spoon and place on a paper towel. To serve, place two potato pancakes atop fresh baby spinach. Add two poached eggs and top with a large spoonful of warm sauce. Garnish with fresh chopped chives.

Poached Eggs Served *in a* Roasted Tomato *with* Goat Cheese

I like to serve this with toasted ciabatta or focaccia bread for dipping.

Serves 4

4 small ripe tomatoes, halved

4 tablespoons extra virgin olive oil

1 tablespoon granulated sugar

salt

freshly ground black pepper

1/4 cup white vinegar

8 extra-large eggs

8 ounces goat cheese

one (10-ounce) package of fresh baby spinach

2 tablespoons fresh chopped chives, for garnish

1 teaspoon smoked paprika

1. Preheat the oven to 350 degrees.

2. Place the tomato halves on baking sheet cut side up. Scoop a very small amount of the center out with a melon baller. Drizzle with olive oil, sugar, salt, and pepper to taste, and roast for about an hour.

3. With ten minutes or so left for the tomatoes, in a shallow sauté pan (2 to 3 quarts), fill 3/4 with water and add the white vinegar. Bring to a slow rolling boil.

4. Crack one egg into a small bowl and lower into the boiling water. Repeat with the next 7 eggs. Cook 3 to 4 minutes (if you like a soft, runny yolk). Remove and place into a bowl of warm water to keep warm.

5. Remove the eggs from warm water with a slotted spoon and place on a paper towel.

6. To serve, place a tablespoon of goat cheese on each tomato. Top it with a poached egg and place it over a bed of baby spinach. Garnish with the chopped chives, some more cracked pepper, and a dash of paprika.

CHAPTER 4

Baked Goods

Mini Banana Bundts

This recipe is so easy that I almost didn't include it. But it's a great way to make something basic into a pretty and delicious treat. If you want to make it particularly fancy, drizzle Dark Chocolate Sauce *(page 136)* on the cakes once they have cooled.

Makes 8 mini-bundts

3/4 cup granulated sugar

1/4 cup light brown sugar

1/2 cup butter, softened

2 tablespoons sour cream

2 large eggs

3 medium-size ripe bananas, mashed

1 tablespoon vanilla

1 3/4 cups cake flour

1 teaspoon baking powder

1/2 teaspoon baking soda

1/4 teaspoon salt

1/2 cup pecans (optional)

1/2 cup mini chocolate chips (optional)

1. Preheat oven to 350 degrees.

2. Coat the mini Bundt pans with butter or vegetable oil.

3. Combine the sugars, butter, and sour cream and mix on medium speed until well combined. Add the eggs and continue to mix until smooth. Add the mashed banana and the vanilla and mix another few seconds to combine.

4. Fold in the flour, baking powder, baking soda, and salt and mix on low speed until just blended. Be careful not to overmix it. Fold in the pecans and/or chocolate chips, if using, and pour into the molds.

5. Bake for 25 minutes in mini Bundt molds. If you don't have mini Bundt molds and are using a regular pan, bake for 40 to 45 minutes.

Dana's Gourmet Granola

We used to package and sell this to the local market in Southwest Harbor but were unable to keep up with the demand while the inn was open during the peak season. We offered this to our guests every morning with fruit and yogurt before the plated fruit course and entrée. This is actually the first time I've parted with my recipe.

Makes approximately 5 cups

1/2 cup canola oil

1/4 cup honey

1 teaspoon cinnamon

1 teaspoon vanilla extract

2 cups thick cut oats (not quick cooking)

3/4 cup shredded coconut

3/4 cup sliced almonds

1/2 cup pecans

1/2 cup pumpkin seeds

1/2 cup dried cranberries

1/2 cup golden raisins

1. Preheat the oven to 325 degrees. Line a rimmed baking sheet with parchment paper.

2. Combine the oil and honey in a small glass mixing cup and microwave for 90 seconds. Add the vanilla and cinnamon and set aside.

3. In a large mixing bowl combine the oats, coconut, almonds, pecans, pumpkin seeds, cranberries, and raisins and mix well. Add the oil and honey mixture and mix with spatula until very well coated.

4. Spread the granola onto a baking sheet and bake until just lightly browned, about 25 to 30 minutes, stirring halfway through to ensure even cooking.

5. Store in an airtight container in the pantry for up to 1 week. The cooked granola freezes very well and keeps for a couple months.

Chocolate-Dipped Coconut Macaroons

By now you might have realized that I have an affinity for chocolate! These are double chocolate with cocoa folded into the egg white and coconut mixture. Why? Because a girl can never have too much chocolate. Again, everything in moderation.

Makes about 36

4 egg whites

3/4 cup granulated sugar

1 teaspoon vanilla extract

2 tablespoons cocoa powder

6 tablespoons flour

5 cups shredded coconut

1 cup mini chocolate chips

2 cups chocolate melting wafers

I. Preheat the oven to 300 degrees.

2. In a large bowl, beat the egg whites with the sugar and vanilla until frothy, about 2 minutes.

3. Add the cocoa powder and flour and stir until combined. Then beat again for about 30 seconds to 1 minute.

4. Fold in coconut and chocolate chips and mix to coat completely.

5. Using a large cookie dough scoop, place spoonfuls onto a parchment- or silicone-lined baking sheet and bake for 20 to 25 minutes until the edges are just lightly browned.

6. While the cookies are cooling, melt the chocolate wafers in a small bowl in the microwave, for 1 1/2 to 2 minutes, stirring after 1 minute, then again after another 30 seconds to see if they're fully melted. Dip each macaroon halfway into melted chocolate and let harden on a sheet of wax paper.

CHOCOLATE-DIPPED
COCONUT MACAROONS,
page 83

Cinnamon Buns

Cinnamon has to be one of the best aromas given off during baking. This was a recipe that I had to play with several times to get the right combination of soft, chewy dough and gooey filling.

Makes 10 large buns

Dough

1 package dry yeast

¼ cup warm water (105 to 110 degrees)

½ cup whole milk, warmed

½ cup granulated sugar

½ stick unsalted butter, softened

1 egg

1 tablespoon vanilla extract

½ teaspoon salt

3 cups flour

Filling

½ cup golden raisins

¾ cup dark brown sugar

½ stick unsalted butter, melted

1 tablespoon cinnamon

¼ teaspoon nutmeg

½ cup pecans (optional)

Glaze

1¹/₂ cups powdered sugar

5 tablespoons milk

2 tablespoons cream cheese, at room temperature

1 tablespoon vanilla extract

I. To make the dough, mix the yeast with water in a large bowl and let sit until dissolved, 5 to 10 minutes. Add the warm milk, sugar, butter, egg, vanilla, and salt, and mix until incorporated. Transfer to a stand mixer fitted with the dough hook. Add the flour and turn on low speed, scraping down after a minute. Increase to medium-low and knead for about 6 to 8 minutes, or until the dough is elastic. Cover the bowl with plastic wrap and a towel and let it sit in a warm place to rise for an hour and fifteen minutes.

2. Prepare the filling by mixing together the raisins, sugar, butter, cinnamon, nutmeg, and nuts in a medium bowl.

3. Line a sheet pan with parchment paper or a silicone liner.

4. Roll out the dough on a floured surface into a rectangle about 10x13, side to side. Brush the dough with the melted butter and sprinkle the filling evenly. Roll up away from your body, starting with the edge closest to you (as if rolling into a log or a jelly roll). Make sure when you finish rolling, you keep the seam side down. Cut into ten even sections. Place each piece, cut side up, onto the sheet pan.

5. Allow them to rise a second time for an hour and a half in a warm spot or on the proof setting in your oven (about 80 degrees).

6. Preheat the oven to 350 degrees.

7. Bake the buns for 18 to 20 minutes, until just very lightly golden brown.

8. Meanwhile, to make the glaze, mix together the sugar, milk, cream cheese, and vanilla in a small bowl. Drizzle it over the warm buns. Serve warm and enjoy! If you manage not to eat them all, keep them in an airtight container and microwave for 10 seconds when you're ready to eat.

Pecan Shortbread

These are an adaptation from my mother-in-law's Pecan Puffs. They're wonderful with a cup of tea or coffee in the afternoon, though not bad at breakfast, either.

Makes about 18 bars

2 sticks unsalted butter, softened
1/3 cup granulated sugar
2 teaspoons vanilla extract
2 cups finely ground pecans
2 cups flour
powdered sugar, for garnish

1. Preheat the oven to 300 degrees.

2. Cream together the butter and sugar with a mixer until smooth. Add the vanilla, pecans, and flour, and stir gently until fully combined.

3. Press the mixture into a glass baking dish coated with butter.

4. Bake for about 25 to 30 minutes, until just lightly browned. Remove from the oven, let cool 2 to 3 minutes, then cut into squares and let fully cool in the pan.

5. Once cool, sprinkle the powdered sugar on top and decorate with a pecan half.

White Chocolate Chip Pecan Cookies

This is my version of a Pecan Sandie. I used to make these at the inn with macadamia nuts and they were always a favorite. Any nuts can be used. There was a very special elderly couple who stayed at our inn several times. They referred to these cookies as "theirs," so I'd send a batch to them at holiday time. It's amazing what the memory of a simple little cookie can do for the soul. And for the person giving them.

Makes about 36 cookies

1²/₃ cups flour

³/₄ teaspoon baking powder

¹/₂ teaspoon baking soda

¹/₂ teaspoon salt

³/₄ cup light brown sugar

¹/₃ cup granulated sugar

1 tablespoon vanilla extract

1¹/₂ sticks unsalted butter, softened

1 large egg

1¹/₂ cups white chocolate chips

1 cup shredded coconut

³/₄ cups chopped pecans or macadamias

1. Preheat the oven to 325 degrees.

2. Combine the flour, baking powder, baking soda, and salt and set aside.

3. In a mixing bowl, combine the sugars, vanilla, and butter and mix on medium speed until blended. Add the egg and continue mixing until smooth. Add the flour mixture and blend on low speed for about 10 seconds. Fold in the white chocolate chips, coconut, and nuts.

4. Scoop out onto a parchment- or silicone-lined baking sheet.

5. Bake 10 to 12 minutes, until just lightly browned. For chewy cookies, bake 9 to 10 minutes; for crispy cookies bake, 12 to 13 minutes.

Triple Chocolate Malted Cookies

I call these Chocolate Dreams! Adding Nutella and malt powder keeps them moist and chewy. Triple chocolatey, actually. They're crisp on the outside and chewy on the inside—for me that's the best way to enjoy them!

Makes about 42 cookies

2 1/4 cups flour

3/4 teaspoon baking powder

1/2 teaspoon baking soda

1/4 teaspoon salt

3/4 cup dark brown sugar

1/3 cup granulated sugar

1/2 cup malted milk powder

1 cup cocoa powder

1 tablespoon vanilla extract

1 cup Nutella

2 sticks unsalted butter, softened

2 large eggs

1 1/2 cups semi-sweet chocolate chips

1. Preheat the oven to 350 degrees.

2. Combine the flour, baking powder, baking soda, and salt and set aside.

3. In mixing bowl, combine the sugars, malt powder, cocoa powder, vanilla, Nutella, and butter and mix on medium speed until blended. Add the eggs and mix until smooth. Add the flour mixture and mix on low for 6 to 8 seconds. Fold in the chocolate chips.

4. Scoop out onto parchment- or silicone-lined baking sheet.

5. Bake for 10 to 12 minutes, until just lightly browned. These cookies will set up once cool, but you'll want to pull them out of the oven before they're firm to the touch.

Dana's Tip

For regular chocolate chip cookies with malt powder,
just eliminate the Nutella and cocoa powder.

Chocolate Cherry Cordial Tart

Wonderful as an afternoon treat with coffee or tea.
Add a scoop of vanilla bean ice cream and you have a perfect dessert.

Serves 8

4 cups fresh sweet Bing cherries, pitted

$^1/_2$ cup sugar

$^1/_4$ cup port wine

1 tablespoon chocolate balsamic
  vinegar (I use Fiore), but if not
  available, use an aged Balsamic

1 teaspoon arrow root powder
  (dissolved in a couple
  tablespoons of the port)

2 teaspoons cocoa powder

1 sheet frozen puff pastry,
  thawed

4 ounces softened cream cheese

4 ounces shaved chocolate (or
  chips)

I. Preheat the oven to 375 degrees.

2. Mix the pitted cherries with the sugar, port,
   balsamic, dissolved arrow root powder, and cocoa
   and put into medium saucepan. Cook over medium
   heat until sauce comes to a boil. Remove cherries and boil
   sauce 2 to 3 minutes longer to thicken. Remove from heat and
   place cherries back into sauce and allow to rest.

3. Press the puff pastry sheet into a 9-inch shallow and greased baking dish or tart
   pan.

4. Spread the softened cream cheese on the pastry. Spread the chocolate shavings
   (or chips) evenly over the cream cheese. And using a slotted spoon, place the
   cherries in a single layer over chocolate.

5. Bake for 35 minutes. Allow to cool at least 20 minutes before serving.

Chewy Cranberry Oatmeal Cookies

This is a twist on the classic oatmeal raisin cookie. This was another favorite of our guests. I use a touch of orange juice and cranberry juice to soften the cranberries before adding them to the batter. For the classic, I use golden raisins as they seem more moist to me.

Makes about 36 cookies

1 cup cranberries

1 cup orange juice

½ cup cranberry juice

2 sticks butter, softened

1 cup packed brown sugar

½ cup granulated sugar

2 large eggs

1 teaspoon baking soda

1 teaspoon vanilla extract

¼ teaspoon salt

1 teaspoon cinnamon

3 cups medium-cut oats (not quick cooking)

1¾ cups flour

1. Combine the cranberries, orange juice, and cranberry juice in a small bowl and let sit for an hour.

2. Preheat the oven to 350 degrees.

3. In a mixing bowl, combine the butter and sugars on medium speed until well blended. Add the eggs and mix until smooth. Add the baking soda, vanilla, salt, and cinnamon and combine. Add the oats and mix until just blended.

4. Drain the cranberries and fold into the batter. Add the flour and mix for another 3 to 5 seconds on low speed until just blended.

5. Drop rounded tablespoons of the dough onto a parchment- or silicone-lined baking sheet about 2 inches apart. Bake for 10 minutes, until the edges are lightly browned.

Blueberry White Chocolate Chip Cookies

These are a soft, moist, almost muffin-like cookies made with the addition of sour cream. The short story and inspiration behind this cookie? It was the result of a blueberry sour cream coffee cake gone bad. Stuck to the pan so bad that it didn't even resemble a cake! The next try was in the form of these individual cookies, which was far more successful.

Makes about 36 cookies

1 stick unsalted butter, softened

3/4 cup sour cream

1/3 cup granulated sugar

3/4 cup packed brown sugar

1 egg

1/2 teaspoon baking soda

1/2 teaspoon baking powder

1 tablespoon vanilla extract

1/4 teaspoon salt

1 cup medium-cut oats (not quick cooking)

2 cups flour

1 cup white chocolate chips

1 cup fresh Maine blueberries (if frozen, allow to thaw and drain)

1. Preheat the oven to 350 degrees.

2. In a mixing bowl, combine the butter, sour cream, and sugars and beat on medium speed until well blended. Add the egg and mix until smooth.

3. Add baking soda, baking powder, vanilla, and salt to the mixture and combine.

4. Fold in the oats, then the flour and mix until just blended. Fold in the white chocolate chips and the blueberries.

5. Drop rounded tablespoons of dough onto a parchment- or silicone-lined baking sheet about 2 inches apart. Bake for 10 to 12 minutes, until puffed and barely dry to the touch. Try not to allow the cookies to brown.

Dana's Tip

It wasn't until the 1840s that the blueberry was harvested in Maine commercially. There are more than 60,000 acres of wild blueberry fields in Maine—a huge contribution to Maine's economy. This tiny berry is high in antioxidants and flavor.

Chocolate Almond Toffee

I have a long story behind the success of this recipe and it involves not making it when you're waiting for guests to check in. Let's just say I was mere seconds from starting a fire in my kitchen. Do not attempt to combine any other task when working with sugar and heat. Don't answer the phone, don't give the dog a treat, don't step away from the stove. Do as I say, not as I do. Read and repeat.

Makes 2½ pounds

1 cup whole almonds

1 cup sliced almonds

2 sticks unsalted butter

1 cup granulated sugar

6 tablespoons corn syrup

2 cups chocolate chips

I. Preheat the oven to 350 degrees.

2. Toast the whole almonds and sliced almonds separately on small baking sheets until fragrant and lightly browned, about 15 minutes. Let cool.

3. Line another baking sheet with parchment paper and set aside.

4. Chop the whole nuts in a processor until coarsely chopped. Set aside half of the nuts. Continue to process the rest of the whole nuts until finely chopped. Use these for the topping.

5. Combine the butter, sugar, and corn syrup in a saucepan and cook over medium heat until melted. Increase the heat so that the sugar slowly boils until it is the color of light caramel. This step is very important as caramel takes a while to turn, but once it gets closer to that point it can overcook and burn very quickly. You'll want to make sure you remove it from the heat the very second you see a drop of smoke or well before, if the color is right. On a candy thermometer (if you trust yours), cook the caramel until it reaches 290 degrees.

6. Remove from heat and fold in the sliced almonds and half of the coarsely chopped almonds and quickly stir to combine as the mixture will harden fast. Pour the mixture

onto the parchment-lined baking sheet and spread with an offset spatula to create an even thickness as best you can. It's okay if the toffee does not fill the entire pan.

7. Top with the chocolate chips and let sit for 1 minute to melt. Spread with the offset spatula. Then toss the remaining finely chopped nuts on top and refrigerate until cool and completely set, about 2 hours. Let the toffee sit at room temperature for 30 minutes or so before breaking into pieces. Store in an airtight container. Freezes beautifully and tastes delicious right out of the freezer. Keeps for a couple months in the freezer if you can manage not to eat it before then!

Chocolate Banana Bread Cookies

These are a fun way to use ripe bananas other than the classic banana bread. They're a cross between a cookie and banana bread; not too sweet, but dipping them in chocolate certainly takes care of that!

Makes 26 to 30

1½ sticks unsalted butter, softened

¾ cup dark brown sugar

⅓ cup granulated sugar

1 large egg

1 very ripe banana, mashed

1 cup thick-cut oats (not quick cooking)

½ teaspoon baking soda

¾ teaspoon baking powder

¼ teaspoon salt

1 teaspoon cinnamon

1½ cups flour

¾ cup mini chocolate chips

½ cup chopped walnuts (optional)

2 cups chocolate melting wafers

I. Preheat the oven to 375 degrees.

2. In a large mixing bowl, combine the butter and sugars and beat on medium speed until well blended Add the egg and banana and mix until smooth.

3. Fold in the oats, baking soda, baking powder, salt, and cinnamon and mix well. Add the flour and mix just until blended. Fold in the chips and nuts (if using).

4. Drop by small scoopfuls onto parchment- or silicone-lined baking sheet and bake for 12 to 14 minutes, until puffed and dry to the touch, but not browned.

5. While the cookies are cooling, melt the chocolate wafers in a small bowl in the microwave, for 1 ½ to 2 minutes, stirring after 1 minute, then again after another 30 seconds to see if they're fully melted. Dip each cookie halfway into the melted chocolate and let harden on a sheet of wax paper.

Chocolate Truffles

These decadent, rich little morsels were something I made before we moved to Maine to buy the B&B. I thought I would continue the tradition of giving them to family and friends to our guests at the inn. I bought small individual covered candy dishes and placed two small truffles in the dish every day. During the warmer months I'd replace them with my Chocolate Rum Balls *(page 103)* since they have a cookie base and hold up to warmer weather better than the truffles.

Makes about 50

2 cups plus 2 tablespoons dark or semi-sweet chocolate chips

2/3 cup heavy cream

2 tablespoons Grand Marnier, raspberry liqueur, Kahlua or dark rum (whatever your flavor preference)

1. Place the chocolate chips in a medium mixing bowl.
2. Bring the heavy cream to a low boil in a small saucepan and remove about 10 seconds after it begins to boil. Add the liqueur and mix.
3. Pour the hot cream mixture over the chocolate chips and stir until melted.
4. Refrigerate until set enough to roll, about two hours.
5. Roll a small teaspoonful into small balls and dip into your coating of choice. Set on a wax paper lined tray and refrigerate when all are rolled.

Coating Options:

1/2 cup powdered sugar

1/2 cup cocoa powder

1 cup mini chocolate chips

1/2 cup non-pareils

1/2 cup sprinkles

Sour Cream Coffee Cake

This recipe is inspired by my mom. At each family holiday dinner or gathering we'd ask Mom to make her wonderful coffee cake if she hadn't already thought about it. She knew better. This is also something that you can turn into muffins simply by using muffin tins. It's a versatile recipe for breakfast, afternoon baked goods, or dessert. When my eight-year-old niece Allison visited us at the inn several years ago, she saw my husband take the muffins out of the oven for me, assuming that he made the muffins, hence Uncle Greg's nickname, "the muffin man"!

Serves 10 to 14

2 sticks plus 1 tablespoon unsalted butter, softened

2 cups granulated sugar

1 cup sour cream

2 eggs

1 tablespoon vanilla extract

2 cups flour

$1/4$ teaspoon salt

1 teaspoon baking powder

1 teaspoon cinnamon

3 tablespoons dark brown sugar

3 tablespoons chopped pecans

1. Preheat the oven to 350 degrees.

2. Combine the two sticks of butter and sugar in a mixer and beat with a paddle attachment for about a minute. Add the sour cream and eggs and mix until smooth. Fold in the vanilla, flour, salt, and baking powder. Pour just under half of the batter into a well-greased Bundt pan.

3. Melt the remaining tablespoon of butter. Mix it together with the cinnamon, brown sugar, and pecans, Pour the mixture on top of the batter in the center. Layer the remaining batter.

4. Bake for 50 to 60 minutes, until a toothpick comes out clean. Allow to cool completely before removing from the pan. (If you're making muffins, reduce the baking time to 30 to 35 minutes.)

Chocolate French-Style Macaroons

During a visit back to Maryland last year, my mom and I had lunch and then strolled by a French bakery with these little gems in the window. After a taste, I knew I had to come home and make them. American "macaroons" are often made with coconut. But real "macarons" are just egg whites and sugar, similar to meringues. These are filled with Nutella. Being gluten-free, they make a great option for everyone to enjoy. If you're looking for a more traditional macaroon, skip the cocoa powder. Try using ground pistachios instead, and fill the cookies with buttercream frosting in place of the Nutella.

Makes about 18

1¹⁄₂ cups whole almonds

1¹⁄₂ cups powdered sugar

3 extra-large egg whites

¹⁄₈ teaspoon salt

3 tablespoons cocoa powder

¹⁄₈ cup granulated sugar

1 small jar Nutella

1. Preheat the oven to 300 degrees.

2. In a large bowl, combine the almonds and the powdered sugar.

3. In a food processor, grind the whole almonds until very finely ground, yielding about 1 ¹⁄₄ cups.

4. Using a stand mixer, combine the egg whites, salt, and cocoa powder and beat on medium-high speed for a few minutes until very soft peaks form. Add the granulated sugar and beat on high again until stiff peaks form.

5. Fold in the almond mixture and carefully combine, trying not to deflate the egg whites too much.

6. Fill a pastry bag with mixture. If you don't have a pastry bag, snip the corner of a large plastic zipper bag. Pipe 1 ¹⁄₂-inch diameter circles onto parchment- or silicone-lined baking sheets, a couple inches apart.

7. Bake for about 20 minutes. Turn the oven off and let sit another 5 minutes before removing to cool.

8. To fill, place about a teaspoon of Nutella on the bottom of one cookie, using caution not to break as they are fragile, and sandwich it together with another.

9. Dust the tops with powdered sugar. Store in an airtight container for up to 7 days.

Chocolate Rum Balls

Our signature at the Kingsleigh—we put these in all guest rooms on a daily basis. These are reminiscent of fudge, truffle, and brownie, all combined into one. They also hold up in warm summer months because they're a cookie base, which makes them safe for picnics. I used to have my wonderful housekeepers help me roll triple batches just to keep up with the demand!

Makes about 30

8 ounces bittersweet or semi-sweet chocolate

1/2 cup dark or spiced rum

3 tablespoons corn syrup

2 1/2 cups finely ground Oreo cookies

1/2 cup granulated sugar

1. Melt the chocolate with the rum and corn syrup in small saucepan over low heat.

2. Remove from the heat, and add the ground cookie crumbs, mixing thoroughly to combine. Allow the mixture to set up at room temperature for a few hours or in the refrigerator for about an hour.

3. Roll into 1 1/2-inch balls, then dip into a bowl with the granulated sugar to coat, and set on sheet pan or flat plate to chill in the refrigerator until ready to serve. Keep in an airtight container in the refrigerator for 2 weeks or freezer for 2 months.

CHOCOLATE FRENCH-
STYLE MACAROONS,
page 102

Classic Popovers *with* Pineapple Cherry Jam

I used to make these whenever we'd have family over for brunch before we moved, and I continued the tradition for our inn guests. Jordan Pond House in Acadia National Park does make some great popovers and their recipe is very close to mine, but our guests said mine hold their own. On a technical note: Popover pans are designed specifically with a lip that forces the popover up and out to expand, providing its signature balloon-shaped top. Make more than you think you need as your guests will be happy to enjoy more than one. These are for you, Dad.

Makes 12 to 14

4 large eggs

2 cups whole milk

2 cups flour

1 teaspoon salt

Pineapple Cherry Jam *(page 135)*

1. Preheat the oven to 400 degrees.

2. Mix the eggs, milk, flour, and salt in a blender until smooth, scraping down the sides to incorporate all of the flour.

3. Pour the batter into a greased popover pan, filling each indent ¾ of the way. Bake for 20 minutes. Reduce the heat to 350 degrees and bake for another 10 minutes or until the top and edges around the rim are brown.

Dana's Tip

Do not open the oven at all during cooking to avoid the popovers deflating. If you remove them before the sides have browned enough, they won't hold the weight of the crown and will fall, usually to one side. Don't get discouraged, it just takes practice to get them right. But the journey to perfection is delicious nonetheless!

Classic Cream Scones

Cream scones are a cross between a classic scone and a light cake. They're not quite as crumbly with the addition of heavy cream. These are my favorite and really seemed to appeal to our inn guests as well.

Serves 6 to 8

1/4 cup plus 2 tablespoons granulated sugar

1 stick unsalted butter, softened

1/2 cup plus one tablespoon heavy cream

2 eggs

2 cups flour

1/4 teaspoon salt

2 teaspoons baking powder

1 teaspoon vanilla extract

1 tablespoon heavy cream

2 tablespoons raw or turbinado sugar

I. Preheat the oven to 350 degrees.

2. Cream together the sugar and butter in a mixer until combined. Add 1/2 cup of the cream and one egg and continue to mix until smooth. Add the flour, salt, baking powder, and vanilla, and mix until just incorporated.

3. Roll the mixture out on a floured surface into a circle about 1/2- to 3/4-inch thick. Cut into 6 to 8 wedges. Place the wedges on a parchment- or silicone-lined baking sheet. In a small bowl, mix together the remaining egg and tablespoon of heavy cream. Brush the mixture on top of the wedges and then sprinkle with the raw sugar. Bake for 15 minutes, until lightly browned.

Dana's Tip
You could really flavor these any way, just use your imagination. Lemon and ginger cream scones might be nice with a cup of tea, just add 1/2 teaspoon grated ginger (or dry ground) and the zest from one lemon. Or fold in 1/2 cup blueberries or cranberries and add one or two swipes of lemon zest.

Maple Pecan Lace Cookies

This is a cross between a cookie and toffee, more the latter. These can be sandwiched with a flavored buttercream or Nutella filling and they're even more heavenly!

Makes about 20

$^1/_2$ stick unsalted butter

$^1/_4$ cup granulated sugar

3 tablespoons maple syrup

1 tablespoon light brown corn syrup

1 teaspoon maple-flavored extract (vanilla if you don't have maple)

1 cup coarsely chopped pecans

$^1/_2$ cup plus 1 tablespoon flour

I. Preheat the oven to 325 degrees.

2. In a small saucepan, melt the butter and add the sugar, maple syrup, and corn syrup, stirring over low heat until smooth. Add the vanilla, pecans, and flour and stir until well combined.

3. Drop tablespoons of the dough onto parchment- or silicone-lined baking sheet, at least 3 inches apart and bake for 11 to 12 minutes, until caramel brown. The cookies will spread so you may have to push the edges inward with a spatula. Allow to cool for at least 3 to 4 minutes before moving to a cooling rack. Repeat with the remaining dough.

CHAPTER 5

Side Dishes
and
Garnishes

Roasted Fennel Bulbs

I will admit, this vegetable is not for everyone what with its licorice-flavor profile. But caramelize it with garlic-infused olive oil and some of your guests might just change their minds. It makes a great accompaniment to eggs, particularly topped with freshly shaved Parmesan cheese.

Serves 4

2 fennel bulbs

$1/4$ cup extra virgin olive oil

3 cloves garlic, smashed

1 teaspoon coarse kosher salt

$1/2$ teaspoon freshly ground black pepper

4 ounces Parmesan cheese

1 lemon, for garnish

I. Preheat the oven to 375 degrees.

2. Halve each fennel bulb vertically, keeping the core intact to hold the bulb together while roasting.

3. In a small saucepan, add the olive oil and smashed garlic and cook over medium-low heat for 5 minutes. Remove garlic and drizzle the olive oil all over the bulbs. Sprinkle with salt and pepper. Roast the fennel cut side down on baking sheet until caramelized and brown, about 45 minutes, covering with foil after 30 minutes.

4. To serve, cut and remove the core (following the V shape of the core). Using a vegetable peeler, shave a few shards of Parmesan on top of each bulb and serve with a lemon wedge.

Chilled Asparagus *with* Curry Lime Aioli

This steamed and chilled asparagus is delicious dressed with olive oil and lemon, but I love it with this simple curried mayonnaise; most of our guests were pleasantly surprised, too, at this combination of flavors. Why not enjoy fresh vegetables at breakfast? You could serve a few spears with a ramekin of the aioli or put the aioli in a squeeze bottle and serve with a drizzle over the top of a small bunch of the steamed asparagus.

Serves 4

1 cup mayonnaise

1 tablespoon honey

1 teaspoon yellow curry powder

juice of ¹/₂ a lime

¹/₂ teaspoon salt

1 bunch of asparagus, bottoms trimmed

1. Combine the mayonnaise, honey, curry powder, lime juice, and salt in a food processor until smooth (you could mix this by hand, just be sure to mix thoroughly). Refrigerate for 8 hours or overnight before serving. This allows the flavors to meld.

2. Lay the asparagus flat on a plate, cover with a wet paper towel, and microwave for 2 minutes. Let cool and refrigerate overnight.

3. Serve the chilled asparagus with the chilled aioli and a lime wedge.

Dana's Tip
Fresh asparagus should have tight tips without a sign of dryness or even sliminess. To keep them fresh if you aren't using them right away, remove rubber band and place stalks in a tall container with an inch or so of cold water and place a loosely fitting plastic bag over the top and store in the refrigerator. Change the water each day until you use them.

Marsala-Glazed Carrots *with* Butter, Dill, *and* Cranberries

For those of you who raise your eyebrows and think "carrots for breakfast?" Why not? We eat other vegetables for breakfast. A side dish doesn't always have to mean hash browns, bacon, or sausage. Think outside the breakfast box!

Serves 2 to 3

1 pound bag of carrots

1/4 stick butter

1 tablespoon olive oil

1 teaspoon fresh dill weed (1/2 if dried)

1/4 cup dry marsala or dry sherry

1/2 cup dried cranberries

a couple of sprigs fresh flat-leaf parsley

salt, to taste

freshly ground black pepper, to taste

1. Peel the carrots and slice on a diagonal, about 1/4-inch thick.

2. In a large sauté pan, melt the butter, add the olive oil, and cook the carrots and dill, covered, over medium heat, for about 10 minutes.

3. Add the marsala or sherry and the cranberries and cook uncovered for another 5 minutes. Chop the parsley leaves and add to the carrots. Add salt and pepper as desired.

114

MARSALA-GLAZED
CARROTS *with* BUTTER,
DILL, *and* CRANBERRIES,
page 113

Roasted Potato Wedges
with Horseradish Sour Cream

The key to getting a crispy potato outside with a creamy center is soaking them in salt water the night before and baking them on high heat in olive oil. You won't miss fries!

Serves 4

1 tablespoon plus 1 teaspoon salt

2 large baking potatoes, scrubbed, not peeled

1/4 cup extra virgin olive oil

1 teaspoon granulated garlic

2 tablespoons grated Parmesan cheese

1 pint sour cream

1 tablespoon bottled horseradish

1 tablespoon Dijon mustard

2 tablespoons chopped fresh chives

1. Dissolve 1 tablespoon salt in 4 cups of warm water in a large bowl.

2. Cut the potatoes lengthwise into 8 wedges and add to the salt water. Refrigerate overnight, or 8 hours prior to baking.

3. When ready to bake, preheat the oven to 400 degrees.

4. Drain the potatoes thoroughly. Add 1/2 teaspoon salt, olive oil, garlic, and grated Parmesan to the potatoes and toss to coat. Spread on a rimmed baking sheet and bake until browned, about 45 minutes.

5. While the potatoes are baking, mix the sour cream, horseradish, mustard, the remaining 1/2 teaspoon salt, and chives and set aside until ready to serve.

Curry Butter Roasted Delicata Squash

I buy my fall squash at J&P Farm Stand in Ellsworth, Maine. This is one of the few squash varieties with a skin thin enough to eat. This squash is delicious baked in slices, and if cut thin enough, they get crispy outside, almost like squash fries.

Serves 4

1 large delicata squash

4 tablespoons butter

1 tablespoon olive oil

1 teaspoon yellow curry powder

1/4 teaspoon salt

I. Preheat the oven to 350 degrees.

2. Halve the squash and remove the seeds. Slice into 1/2-inch slices and place on a rimmed baking sheet.

3. Melt the butter with the olive oil in microwave for 60 seconds. Add the curry powder and salt and mix well. Pour the mixture over the squash and bake until tender, 25 to 30 minutes, turning halfway through cooking. Top with a small pat of the Curried Butter *(page 144)*.

Salmon *and* Cucumber Roulade

I like to use salmon from Sullivan Harbor in Sullivan, Maine. This makes a nice small accompaniment to an entrée. It's much more than just a beautiful garnish. You can omit the cucumber in this roulade.

Serves 4

1 medium cucumber

eight (1-inch wide) slices of smoked salmon, about 5 inches long

4 tablespoons cream cheese, softened at room temperature

4 pieces red or green-leaf lettuce

1 lemon, thinly sliced, for garnish

1 fresh dill sprig, chopped (about 1 tablespoon)

juice of 1 lemon, for drizzling over top of salmon

1. Peel the cucumber and cut to 6 inches in length. Using the peeler, shave 8 thin strips of cucumber from end to end and place each on a paper towel to absorb the moisture.

2. Place a slice of salmon on top of each cucumber slice.

3. Spread 1 tablespoon of the cream cheese on top of each slice of salmon.

4. Roll up and stand vertically, on edge, revealing the cut edge.

5. When ready to plate, place a small piece of lettuce, top with two salmon roulades, side by side, separated by a thin lemon slice. Add a sprinkle of dill and freshly squeezed lemon over the salmon.

Roasted Tomato *and* Swiss Tart

Another wonderful appetizer, but we served this as a decadent accompaniment to eggs at the inn. It would also make a lovely lunch. Pastry, cheese, and tomatoes together? I'm happy.

Serves 8

6 plum tomatoes, halved

2 tablespoons olive oil

1/4 teaspoon salt

a few turns of freshly ground black pepper

1 package refrigerated pie dough

1 egg

1 cup ricotta cheese

2 cloves garlic, finely chopped

1/4 cup grated Parmesan cheese

1/4 cup shredded Parmesan cheese

1/2 cup shredded Swiss or Jarlsburg cheese

1 small sprig of fresh thyme

1. Preheat the oven to 375 degrees.

2. Place the tomato halves on a baking sheet, sprinkle on the olive oil, salt, and pepper and roast for an hour.

3. Meanwhile, press the pie dough into a 9-inch pie pan coated with non-stick cooking spray. Beat the egg and add a teaspoon of water. Brush the edges of the dough with the egg wash and bake for 15 minutes, remove to fill.

4. Mix the ricotta, garlic, and grated Parmesan together until well blended. Add to the pie crust. Top with the shredded Parmesan and Swiss cheeses. Top with the tomato halves and thyme.

5. Lower the oven to 350 degrees and bake until bubbly and lightly browned, about 25 minutes. Let sit 5 minutes before slicing.

Raw Beets, Jicama, *and* Carrot Salad *with* Goat Cheese, Pecans, and Orange Vinaigrette

This uses the same vinaigrette as the following recipe, but contains raw beets instead. It's one step simpler and raw beets when shredded are nicely tender–crisp.

Serves 4

1 large beet, peeled

2 large carrots, peeled

1/2 medium jicama

1 small shallot, finely chopped

1/4 cup olive oil

1/2 teaspoon pure orange extract

1 tablespoon balsamic vinegar

1/2 teaspoon salt

1/4 teaspoon freshly ground black pepper

6 ounces goat cheese

1/4 cup chopped pecans

1. Using a medium box shredder, grate the beet, carrots, and jicama and place into a mixing bowl.

2. Whisk together the shallot, olive oil, orange extract, vinegar, salt, and pepper. Pour over the grated vegetables.

3. Roll a small scoop of goat cheese into a ball (I use a mini ice cream or cookie dough scoop) and roll into crushed pecans.

4. To serve, place a small portion of the grated beet mixture in the center of a plate. Place a small goat cheese ball on top, and drizzle with a bit more vinaigrette. Finish with a churn of the pepper mill.

Chilled Beets *with* Goat Cheese *and* Orange Vinaigrette

I like to make this featuring goat cheese from Sunset Acres in Brooksville, Maine, and Orange Vinaigrette using Fiore Blood Orange extra virgin olive oil. Use your favorite local goat cheese, and follow the instructions below if you don't have the Fiore oil.

Serves 4 to 6

3 large red beets

6 ounces goat cheese

1/4 cup olive oil

1/2 teaspoon pure orange extract

1 tablespoon balsamic vinegar

salt, to taste

freshly ground black pepper, to taste

2 thyme sprigs

I. Preheat the oven to 375 degrees.

2. Peel the beets and wrap in non-stick foil. Roast in the oven for 45 minutes to 1 hour, until tender. Slice into 1/8 to 1/4 inch rounds when cool.

3. Mix the olive oil and vinegar with a dash of salt, pepper, and the leaves from 1 sprig of thyme.

4. To serve, layer the sliced beets with a tablespoon of goat cheese in between. Drizzle with the vinaigrette and garnish with a few fresh thyme leaves.

Black Pepper Candied Bacon

MAKE EXTRA. PERIOD.

1 pound of thick-cut bacon (I prefer applewood smoked)
light brown sugar
freshly ground black pepper

1. Preheat the oven to 350 degrees.
2. Lay the bacon flat on a rimmed baking sheet. Sprinkle each piece with about ½ teaspoon of the sugar. Add plenty of black pepper straight from a peppermill.
3. Bake until crispy, about 30 minutes. Remove to a piece of foil, or a cotton towel, not paper towel, as the sugar will cause the bacon to stick.

Roasted Heirloom Tomatoes

My favorite seasonal ingredient from Chase's Daily in Belfast, Maine, a beautiful vegetarian restaurant and vegetable market. Roasting and caramelizing brings out the sweetness in most vegetables, and in this case, fruit. These make not only a great side dish but also a wonderful omelet filling or frittata topping. On crostini with goat cheese is one of my favorites that could accompany an egg dish. When I make these, I make a large batch and freeze them in individual portions as they're so versatile.

10 medium-size heirloom tomatoes (all colors if they have them)
½ cup olive oil
1 teaspoon salt
½ teaspoon freshly ground black pepper
1 teaspoon sugar

1. Preheat the oven to 350 degrees.
2. Quarter the tomatoes and place them on a rimmed baking sheet. Sprinkle on the olive oil, salt, pepper, and sugar and roast for an hour. Save the oil/drippings from roasting to make a vinaigrette or use for dipping crusty bread.

Sweet Potato Pancakes

These make a perfect substitute for an English muffin in poached egg dishes. I've used them in this cookbook for Poached Eggs with Creamed Poblano and Shallot Sauce *(page 76)*.

Makes 12 to 14

2 large sweet potatoes

1 medium yellow or sweet onion

3 eggs

3/4 cup flour

1 1/2 teaspoons baking powder

1 teaspoon salt

1/4 teaspoon freshly ground black pepper

1/8 teaspoon yellow curry powder

2 cups vegetable oil for frying (or enough to come up about 1/4 inch from the bottom of the pan)

1. In a food processor using the medium shredding disc, process the potatoes and onion and set into a large mixing bowl.

2. Add the eggs, flour, baking powder, salt, pepper, curry powder and mix until well blended.

3. In a large frying pan, heat vegetable oil until hot. Take about 1/3 cup of the mixture and shape it into a flat disc as best you can, then carefully add to the oil, trying to keep its round shape. Fry for 3 to 4 minutes, until brown on one side. Flip, cooking another 3 minutes until browned. Remove to a paper towel. Repeat until all the pancakes are fried. You can keep them warm in a 250 degree oven until ready to serve.

Savory Spinach
and Parmesan Cheesecake

This is a classic spinach dip in cheesecake form, but with the texture of a quiche. It's great for an afternoon appetizer, light brunch, or lunch with a salad. On occasion at the inn I liked to serve a small slice of this alongside a sweet crepe, sliced crusty bread, or focaccia.

Serves 12

Crust

¾ stick butter, melted

¾ cup Panko bread crumbs

¼ cup shredded Parmesan cheese

Filling

2 shallots, chopped

1 tablespoon olive oil

2 cloves garlic, finely chopped

one (10-ounce) bag fresh baby spinach

1 bunch scallions

4 eggs

three (8-ounce) packages cream cheese, softened

¼ cup sour cream

4 ounces goat cheese

1 tablespoon Dijon mustard

½ teaspoon salt

½ teaspoon freshly ground black pepper

⅛ teaspoon cayenne pepper

1 teaspoon dry mustard

1 cup shredded Parmesan cheese

½ cup grated Parmesan cheese

½ cup shredded Swiss cheese

1. Preheat the oven to 350 degrees.

2. Mix the melted butter with bread crumbs and Parmesan and press into bottom of 9-inch spring form pan. Bake for 10 minutes.

3. Sauté the shallots in the olive oil over medium heat until soft and lightly browned, about 10 minutes. Add the garlic and cook, stirring, for 30 seconds. Remove from the pan and place in a large bowl.

4. Add the spinach to the same pan, cover, and cook over medium-low heat for 3 minutes. Remove, pat dry. Chop and add to the shallots.

5. Chop the scallions and add them to the shallot and spinach mixture.

6. In a mixing bowl, beat the eggs on medium speed. Add the cream cheese, sour cream, goat cheese, mustard, salt, pepper, cayenne, and dry mustard and mix for 10 to 15 seconds until well combined.

7. Add the Parmesan and Swiss cheeses and the spinach mixture to the eggs and mix on low speed for 5 seconds.

8. Pour into the 9-inch spring form pan on top of the cooked bread crumbs and bake for about an hour, until the center is set. Allow to cool for about 10 minutes before slicing.

Smoked Salmon, Caviar, Horseradish Crème Fraiche, *and* Fresh Dill *on* Cucumber *and* Zucchini Rounds

This is a beautiful garnish almost too pretty to eat! It also makes an elegant hors d'oeuvre to enjoy with some bubbly.

Makes 10

1 medium or large cucumber or zucchini

½ cup crème fraiche

1 tablespoon bottled horseradish

2 sprigs fresh dill

¼ teaspoon salt

4 ounces smoked salmon

1 ounce caviar

I. Cut the zucchini or cucumber into ¾ inch rounds. Using a small melon-baller, scoop out the very center, creating shallow cavities for the sour cream to sit in.

2. Mix together the crème fraiche, horseradish, ½ of a sprig of dill, chopped, and salt.

3. Place about ½ teaspoon of the sour cream onto a vegetable round, then roll up a 2-inch piece of salmon and place it on top, add a ½ teaspoon caviar, and a fresh sprig of dill to garnish.

Dana's Tip

Serve these as soon as you put them together as the natural juice from the caviar after a short time will start to seep onto the sour cream and the plate.

CHAPTER 6

Sauces, Syrups,
and
Flavored Butters

Simple Syrup

This syrup can be used in a variety of sauces, sorbets, drinks, and cocktails.

Makes approximately 2¼ cups

2 cups sugar

1½ cups cold water

2 tablespoons white corn syrup

1. Combine the sugar, water, and corn syrup in a medium saucepan and cook over medium-high heat for about 12 minutes, until all the sugar is completely dissolved. Do not allow the syrup to boil.

2. Remove from heat and allow the syrup to cool completely before using.

3. When cool, pour into a container and store in the refrigerator up to three weeks or the freezer for up to 3 months.

Simple Syrup *with* Basil

This versatile syrup can accompany a variety of fruit dishes, desserts, drinks, and cocktails, and adds a nice herbal kick. This is particularly delicious in lemonade, iced tea, or even orange juice!

Makes approximately 2¼ cups

2 cups sugar

1½ cups cold water

2 tablespoons white corn syrup

½ cup packed fresh basil leaves

1. Combine the sugar, water, and corn syrup in medium saucepan and cook over medium-high heat for about 12 minutes, until all the sugar is completely dissolved. Do not allow the syrup to boil.

2. While the sugar is cooking, finely chop the basil and place half in a mesh bag or loose tea steeper and place into the sugar mixture. Set the other half aside.

3. Remove from heat and allow the syrup to cool completely before using.

4. When cool, remove the basil and add the remainder of the fresh basil to the mix.

5. Pour into a container and store in the refrigerator up to three weeks or in the freezer for up to 3 months.

Dana's Tip

If you do not have a mesh bag or tea steeper, just mix the basil with the rest of the ingredients and strain through a fine-mesh sieve when cool.

Simple Syrup *with* **Green Tea** *and* **Fresh Mint**

This versatile syrup can accompany a variety of fruit dishes, desserts, drinks, and cocktails. It's delicious in iced tea, mojitos, or mint juleps! I served this over cantaloupe at the inn.

Makes approximately 2¼ cups

2 cups sugar

1⅓ cups cold water

1 tablespoon white corn syrup

1 green tea bag

½ cup packed fresh mint leaves

I. Combine the sugar, water, and corn syrup in a medium saucepan and cook over medium-high heat for about 12 minutes, until all the sugar is completely dissolved. Do not allow the syrup to boil.

2. While the sugar is cooking, finely chop the mint and place half in a mesh bag or loose tea steeper and place into sugar mixture. Set the other half aside.

3. Remove from heat, add the tea bag, and allow the syrup to cool completely.

4. When cool, remove the mint and tea bag and add the remainder of the fresh mint.

5. Pour into a container and store in the refrigerator up to three weeks or in the freezer for up to 3 months.

Pineapple Cherry Jam

Again, a new recipe was created from leftover pineapple while making my caramelized Pineapple Banana Cairns *(page 16)*.

2 cups pitted Bing cherries

$1/2$ of a fresh pineapple, cored and cubed

1 cup sugar

I. Put the cherries, pineapple, and sugar in a saucepan and cook over medium heat for about 30 minutes. Allow to cool for about 15 minutes.

2. Purée in a blender or food processor. Strain, discarding half of the liquid and mixing the other half back in. The jam will thicken slightly when cool. As simple as that!

Maple-Rum Sauce

A versatile sauce for pancakes, waffles, French toast, poached pears, baked apples, or fresh blueberries. I use this sauce on my Blueberry Oatmeal Streusel French Toast *(pages 46–48)*.

Makes 2 cups

$1^1/2$ cups heavy cream

$1/3$ cup packed dark brown sugar

$1/4$ cup maple syrup

$1/3$ cup plus 3 tablespoons spiced rum

3 teaspoons corn starch

I. Combine the cream, sugar, maple syrup, and $1/3$ cup rum in a medium saucepan and bring to a slow boil over low heat. Dissolve the corn starch in the remaining 3 tablespoons of rum. Whisk in the cornstarch mixture, lower the heat, and cook for another 2 minutes, until thickened. Remove from the heat and serve warm.

2. When cool, store in the refrigerator for a few days or freeze for up to 3 weeks. Simply reheat in the microwave on low to warm.

Rhubarb Sauce

This is delicious with the Cinnamon Baked Oatmeal Cake *(page 38)* but can be used in a variety of other ways as well.

Makes about 2½ cups

4 cups chopped fresh rhubarb

½ cup water

½ cup granulated sugar

1. Cook the rhubarb, water, and sugar in a medium saucepan, covered, for 20 to 25 minutes until soft.

2. Remove from the heat and puree with an immersion blender until smooth. Serve immediately or let cool and refrigerate until ready to use. Warm in the microwave before serving. This can be stored in the refrigerator for up to 3 days or in the freezer for 4 weeks.

Dark Chocolate Sauce

In addition to being drizzled on the Chocolate, Banana, Raspberry Stuffed French Toast *(page 39)*, this sauce is wonderful over fresh berries and ice cream. I also used it to hand-write messages on plates for special occasions. The tricky part is to not microwave it too long (if chilled) so that the writing will be too warm to set up. It takes practice, so be patient!

Makes about 2 cups

1½ cups heavy cream

1 cup dark brown sugar

8 ounces unsweetened chocolate

½ stick unsalted butter

3 tablespoons spiced rum

⅛ teaspoon salt

½ teaspoon vanilla extract

1. Combine the cream, sugar, chocolate, butter, rum, salt, and vanilla in a small saucepan and melt over medium-low heat until the chocolate is completely melted and combined. Use a whisk and stir constantly for best results.

2. Cool completely and store in squeeze bottles in the refrigerator for up to 1 week or in the freezer for 1 month.

Raspberry Coulis

This is a classic that can be served with numerous fruits or desserts. It can also be used in drinks or cocktails. It's very important to strain sauces using seeded fruits.

Makes about 2 cups

one (24-ounce) bag frozen raspberries, thawed, draining most of the visible
  excess liquid

1/2 cup powdered sugar

1 tablespoon fresh lemon juice

I. Combine the raspberries, sugar, and lemon juice in a blender and puree for about 20 seconds. Push through a fine-mesh sieve or a strainer. Store in a plastic airtight container or squeeze bottles in the refrigerator for 4 days or freezer for 4 weeks.

Dana's Tip

For fresh raspberries, use 1 quart of berries, 1/2 cup Simple Syrup (page 132),
1 tablespoon lemon juice and puree and strain as indicated above.

Blackberry Coulis

This mildly tart sauce is best when served with something sweet to balance out the flavors. I serve it with the Cheese Blintz Soufflé *(pages 44–45)* with the Mango Puree *(page 140)*.It would work well over a panna cotta or vanilla yogurt or ice cream.

Makes about 2 cups

one (24-ounce) bag frozen blackberries, thawed, draining most of the visible
  excess liquid

3/4 cup powdered sugar

1 tablespoon fresh lemon juice

I. Combine the blackberries, sugar, and lemon juice in a blender and puree for about 20 seconds. Push through a fine-mesh sieve or a strainer. Store in a plastic airtight container or squeeze bottles in the refrigerator for 4 days or freezer for 4 weeks.

Dana's Tip

For fresh blackberries, use 1 quart of berries, 1/2 cup Simple Syrup (page 132),
1 tablespoon lemon juice and puree and strain as indicated above.

Mango Puree

Makes about 2 cups

6 ripe mangoes, peeled and cut off the pit

¼ cup **Simple Syrup** *(page 132)*

1 tablespoon fresh lemon juice

I. Combine the mango, Simple Syrup, and lemon, in a blender and puree for about 20 seconds. You could strain this sauce as well, as it is a bit fibrous; I like it a bit thicker so that when I design a plate using a coulis, which is thinner, the thicker puree holds the coulis in place when drawing on the plate.

2. Store in a plastic airtight container or squeeze bottles in the refrigerator for 4 days or freezer for 4 weeks.

Coconut Lime Crème

This sauce is wonderful on a variety of tropical fruits. I particularly love it with the watermelon and kiwi with a heavy squeeze of fresh lime *(page 15)*. This sauce also freezes well.

Makes about 2 cups

1 pint sour cream

½ cup canned coconut milk

¼ teaspoon coconut extract

½ cup powdered sugar

the zest of 1 lime

I. Combine the sour cream, coconut milk, coconut extract, sugar, and lime zest in a blender and puree for about 10 seconds. Scrape down the sides and blend again for another few seconds. Store in a container in the refrigerator for up to 1 week or in the freezer for 4 weeks.

Cinnamon Crème

Not only is this one of the easiest sauces to accompany fresh fruit you can make, but it's also one that can stand up to the heat of a torch to create the classic brûlée topping. The key is the sour cream—it won't curdle or cook when torched the way a brûlée custard with eggs would. It freezes well, too.

Makes about 2 cups

1 pint sour cream
1 tablespoon ground cinnamon
2 tablespoons honey
1 tablespoon heavy cream
1/3 cup dark brown sugar

I. Combine the sour cream, cinnamon, honey, heavy cream, and brown sugar in a blender and puree for about 10 seconds. Scrape down the sides and blend again for another few seconds. Store in a container in the refrigerator for up to 1 week or in the freezer for about 4 weeks.

Vanilla Bean Crème

This sauce can actually be used with the Grapefruit Brule *(page 12)* in addition to accompanying many fruits or even scones.

Makes about 2 cups

1 pint sour cream
1 tablespoon vanilla extract
the seeds from 1 vanilla bean
2 tablespoons honey
1 tablespoon heavy cream
1/3 cup granulated sugar

I. Combine the sour cream, vanilla extract, vanilla bean, honey, heavy cream, and sugar in a blender and puree for about 10 seconds. Scrape down the sides and blend again for another few seconds. Store in a container in the refrigerator for up to 1 week or in the freezer for about 4 weeks.

Maple Crème

Like the vanilla and cinnamon version, this is versatile for sauces, French toast, ice cream, and drizzled on Port Wine Poached Pears *(page 26)*.

Makes about 2 cups

1 pint sour cream

1 teaspoon pure maple extract

¼ cup Maine maple syrup

¼ cup dark brown sugar

I. Combine the sour cream, maple extract, maple syrup, and brown sugar in a blender and puree for about 10 seconds. Scrape down the sides and blend again for another few seconds. Store in a plastic container or squeeze bottles in the refrigerator for up to 1 week or in the freezer for about 4 weeks.

Fresh Whipped Cream

I used to make whipped cream fresh, as I needed it. But then I found the "Whip-It" brand of a whipped cream charger! Next to the torch, this is my favorite tool. But if you don't have one, here's the classic recipe.

Makes about 4 cups

1 pint heavy whipping cream

½ cup granulated sugar

1 teaspoon vanilla extract

I. In large mixing bowl, add the cream, sugar, and vanilla and beat on high until stiff peaks form, about 4 to 5 minutes. Use caution to check after it starts to get thick, checking after every 10 to 15 seconds of beating. If you overbeat, you'll have to dump the batch as you'll be on your way to churned butter!

Garlic Parmesan Butter

A small drop on fried or poached eggs just adds a perfect little something.

Makes about ½ cup (1 stick)

1 stick unsalted butter, softened
1 tablespoon extra virgin olive oil
1 minced garlic clove
⅛ teaspoon salt

I. In a small bowl, using a rubber spatula, combine the butter, olive oil, garlic, and salt until blended. Roll into a log shape and wrap in plastic. Refrigerate until ready to use. Use slices as you would regular butter. Keeps in refrigerator up to 2 weeks.

Chive and Scallion Butter

This is delicious on eggs and savory popovers or scones.

Makes about ½ cup (1 stick)

1 stick butter, softened
1 tablespoon fresh chopped chives
1 stalk scallion, trimmed 1 inch from each end, thinly sliced into ⅛-inch slices
⅛ teaspoon salt

I. In a small bowl, using a rubber spatula, combine the butter, chives, scallion, and salt until well blended. Roll into a log shape and wrap in plastic. Refrigerate until ready to use. Use slices as you would regular butter. Keeps in refrigerator up to 2 weeks.

Curried Butter

Try this on steamed vegetables, an omelet, or scrambled eggs.

Makes about ½ cup

1 stick unsalted butter, softened

1 teaspoon yellow curry powder

1 teaspoon honey

⅛ teaspoon salt

⅛ teaspoon freshly ground black pepper

I. In a small bowl, using a rubber spatula, combine the butter, curry powder, honey, salt, and pepper until well blended. Roll into a log shape and wrap in plastic. Refrigerate until ready to use. Use slices as you would regular butter. Keeps in refrigerator up to 2 weeks.

Orange Cinnamon Buttercream

This delicious combination is wonderful on popovers, scones, waffles, pancakes or even on the Port Wine Poached Plums *(page 26)*.

Makes about 1½ cups

1 stick unsalted butter, softened

2 cups powdered sugar

1 teaspoon ground cinnamon

1 tablespoon milk

1 tablespoon fresh orange juice

1 tablespoon Fiore Blood Orange Olive Oil

I. In a small bowl, using a rubber spatula, mix the butter, sugar, and cinnamon together in a small bowl. Add the milk, orange juice, and olive oil and mix until smooth. Refrigerate until ready to use. Use slices as you would regular butter. Keeps in refrigerator up to 2 weeks.

Cinnamon Spice Butter

This is great on pancakes, waffles, cream scones, and coffee cake.

Makes about ½ cup

1 stick unsalted butter, softened
2 tablespoons powdered sugar
1 tablespoon ground cinnamon
¼ teaspoon ground cloves

I. In a small bowl, using a rubber spatula, mix together the butter and sugar. Add the cinnamon and cloves and mix until smooth. Refrigerate until ready to use. Use slices as you would regular butter. Keeps in refrigerator up to 2 weeks.

Maple Nutmeg Butter

This is great on pancakes, waffles, and cream scones.

Makes about ½ cup

1 stick unsalted butter, softened
2 tablespoons powdered sugar
2 tablespoons maple syrup
1 teaspoon pure maple extract
¼ teaspoon ground nutmeg
2 tablespoons chopped pecans (optional)

I. In a small bowl, using a rubber spatula, mix together the butter and sugar. Add the maple syrup, maple extract, and nutmeg and mix until smooth. Fold in chopped pecans (optional). Refrigerate until ready to use. Use slices as you would regular butter. Keeps in refrigerator up to 2 weeks.

CHAPTER 7

Guest Gifts
and
Menus

Guest Gifts & Menus

Every so often a guest would mention a special occasion they would be celebrating while staying with us. I noted the occasion on each reservation and offered a little something special to help enhance their stay. Sometimes it would be a plate of chocolate-dipped strawberries with a message written in chocolate, other times a small basket of a dozen customized teabags with a stack of Pecan Shortbread. Sometimes I'd call the restaurant where they were dining that evening and have a dessert sent to them from us. For our regular granola-loving guests, I'd package up a pound of granola with our custom labels and have it waiting in their room upon check-in. Many times it meant shipping a batch of their favorite cookies at holiday time. It's the little things that matter the most.

Fill decorative bags, tins, or boxes with:

- Chocolate Almond Toffee *(pages 96–97)*
- Chocolate Rum Balls *(page 103)*
- Chocolate Truffles *(page 99)*
- Dana's Gourmet Granola *(page 82)*

Package a few tea bags or loose-leaf tea with:

- Pecan Shortbread *(page 88)*
- A small Mason jar of Basil Simple Syrup, wonderful as a sweetener for tea *(pages 132–133)*

Give out your recipes:

■ Attach a recipe card for Blueberry White Chocolate Chip Cookies *(page 95)* to a pint of Maine blueberries

■ A small Mason jar of Pineapple Cherry Jam *(page 135)*, a popover pan, and the recipe for Classic Popovers *(page 106)*

■ A good-quality candy thermometer with the recipe for Chocolate Almond Toffee *(pages 96–97)*

For those special occasions:

■ Serve your guests a plate of chocolate dipped strawberries with a hand-written chocolate message.

■ Add a split of bubbly or a decanter of port wine if you'd like. You can have it waiting for them upon arrival.

■ Line a serving tray with a linen napkin and serve a couple slices of the Savory Spinach and Parmesan Cheesecake *(pages 126–127)* with an assortment of crackers and a bottle of a crisp Sauvignon Blanc, an unoaked Chardonnay, or a Pinot Noir.

For your guests who have to leave before breakfast:

■ Send them off with a to-go package of muffins, granola, and fresh fruit with plastic utensils, paper bowls, and napkins.

Menu Combinations

At the inn I had the never-ending challenge of creating menus without repeating anything during anyone's stay for my self-imposed criteria (unless they requested something). I also tried not to use the same fruits, flavors, or ingredients in any of the dishes each morning. You can see why this presented a challenge. Oh, and I should also add to the task, working around food allergies or intolerances. We started each breakfast with a help-yourself offering of muffins or scones, granola, yogurt, and fresh melon. We then served a plated fruit course followed by an entree, and alternated between savory and sweet each day. Sometimes we'd end with a sorbet. Pairing a fruit course with a sweet entree isn't easy as you don't want to overwhelm your guests with sugar! These were some of the menu combinations that seemed to work well for us.

Grapefruit Brûlée with Vanilla Bean Crème *(page 12)*

Asparagus, Carmelized Shallots, and Goat Cheese Frittata *(pages 66–67)*

Marsala-Glazed Carrots with Butter, Dill, and Cranberries *(page 113)*

Classic Popovers *(page 106)*

Port Wine Poached Pears with Vanilla Bean Crème *(page 26)*

Chocolate, Banana, Raspberry French Toast *(page 39)*

Pineapple Banana Cairns with Cinnamon Crème *(page 16)*

Egg Roulade Filled with Sautéed Leeks and Parmesan, Topped with Lobster, Sherry, and Melted Butter *(pages 58–59)*

Roasted Potato Wedges with Horseradish Sour Cream *(page 116)*

Roasted Plums with Thyme, Honey, and Vanilla Frozen Yogurt *(page 19)*

Chive and Cream Cheese Scrambled Eggs in Wonton Cups *(page 64)*

Roasted Heirloom Tomatoes *(page 124)*

Watermelon and Kiwi with Coconut Lime Crème *(page 15)*

Savory Spinach and Parmesan Cheesecake *(pages 126–27)*

Smoked Salmon Duo: Salmon and Cucumber Roulade (page 118) and Smoked Salmon, Caviar, Horseradish Crème Fraiche, and Fresh Dill on Cucumber and Zucchini Rounds *(page 128)*

Chilled Asparagus with Curry Lime Aioli *(page 112)*

Cinnamon Baked Oatmeal Cake with Warm Rhubarb Sauce *(page 38)*

Blueberry Apricot Cheese Crepes *(pages 36–37)*

Black Pepper Candied Bacon *(page 124)*

Vanilla Bean Panna Cotta with Berries *(page 18)*

Poached Eggs on a Sweet Potato Pancake Topped with Creamed Carmelized Shallots and Poblano Peppers *(page 76)*

Cantaloupe with Green-Tea-Infused Minted Simple Syrup *(page 22)*

Papaya, Mango, and Strawberries with Lemon and Basil *(page 24)*

Ricotta, Butternut Squash, and Zucchini Crepes with Sage Brown Butter *(page 70)*

index

index

index

642 MOO
Moos, Dana
     The art of breakfast : how to brin...

5CLY0016366

DATE DUE			